Is it bedtime yet?

Pro Parenting Tips for
Rank Amateurs

MICHAL MCDOWELL

ILLUMIFY

MEDIA.COM

The views and opinions expressed in this book are those of the author and do not necessarily reflect the official policy or position of Illumify Media Global.

Published by
Illumify Media Global
www.IllumifyMedia.com
"Let's bring your book to life!"

Library of Congress Control Number: 2021916514

Paperback ISBN: 978-1-955043-37-3

Typeset by Jen Clark
Cover design by Debbie Lewis
Front cover photograph by Alima Blackwell or Raven's Nest Photography
Author photograph by Tracy Doty

Printed in the United States of America

This book is dedicated to parents with young ones. I see you.
You've got this!

Contents

Acknowledgments

Thank you to my husband for being my partner in parenthood and for encouraging me to write, and to my sons for cheering me on even though they were the subject matter.

Thank you to all of the other parents in my life who inspired me by their own great parenting skills, especially, Janice Grass, Amy Young, and Caren Matteucci.

Thank you to everyone who said, "You should write a book!"

Thank you, Mom. You get all the credit for how I turned out. Hopefully, that's a good thing. Ha! Also, sorry for the expletives.

Introduction

Let me begin this parenting book by being perfectly clear. I am not an expert. Not in the technical sense. I have no education on child psychology or child development. What I do have is two really great kids.

My sons are almost all adults (well, one is nineteen, but is that really an adult?) and my youngest is seventeen. I am constantly complimented on how great they are. It's been this way most of their childhoods. Could be they were just born this way but . . . I know better. I remember the dark days of constant redirection, toddler fits and crying . . . and that was just me. The kids were a handful too.

I've had so many friends ask me how we did it. How did we handle this problem and that? I usually hand them a book called *Making Your Kids Mind Without Losing Yours* by Dr. Kevin Leman. It's the book that saved my children's lives. It's the book that changed how I parent.

Though I'm so grateful for the expert guidance I got from this doctor's book, it was not the only resource I had. It truly "takes a village" and I'm forever grateful to the other Village Parents in my life who gave me advice and encouragement along the way.

I also think there was a touch of instinct or gift in the area. (We really need a sarcasm font). I started babysitting when I was eleven. (It was the nineties . . . they did stuff like that back then). I was really good at it, though. It was cool to find ways to get kids to mind me without yelling at them or spanking them. (Again, it was the nineties, and these were the go–to parenting techniques of the day.)

So, I'm going to give it a shot. I'm going to write this book of my parenting advice and experience. This is the stuff that worked for me, and I think it could work for you.

Spaghetti or The Second Introduction

Have you ever noticed that almost everyone likes spaghetti, but they don't necessarily like other people's spaghetti as much? Though all the ingredients are pretty much the same, not everyone's spaghetti tastes the same. We all have a sauce preference, whether it's homemade or from a jar, different seasonings, meat or veggies or both. There are even different pastas.

Parenting is the same.

We all use some basic ingredients, but the spices and other additions should be to your liking and what works best for your home, your family, and your unique child. Factors like how you were parented, your religion/absence of religion, your culture, your age, and your child's personality will no doubt contribute to how you parent.

Some of my suggestions won't work for you or they will work for you with your personal modification. Just promise me to have a "no, thank you" bite before you decide it's not to your liking. (If you don't know what a "no, thank you" bite is, continue reading.)

The Goal of Parenting or The Third Introduction

My parenting style has been influenced most by remembering that the goal of parenting has little to do with shaping a child but is all about shaping an *adult*. Your children will not stay children. They will grow up, and they will leave you. Your goal as a parent is not to have a happy kid or a well-behaved child but to raise a functional and responsible *adult*, a person who will be independent of you, not dependent on you.

There are always exceptions to the rule. If your child is differently abled, or if you don't have a parenting partner on the same page as you, or you're a working parent as opposed to a stay-at-home parent . . . all these things and more can affect your parenting. As I said in the beginning, take the ingredients and spices that are working for you, and run with them.

If you're reading this and have older and less malleable kids, it still doesn't mean you can't change your approach. It is much harder after age fifteen, but you can always sit them down and let them know that you want to do things differently as a parent.

I always told my kids, "I'm doing my best, but I know I have and will make mistakes. I hope you'll always be forgiving of it. Hopefully, it will give you a good sense of humor and something to talk to a therapist about."

You are going to mess up. None of us are perfect. We're not, and our kids are not. What I've written here is the good stuff. There's so much I know I've done wrong, but when I look at my kids, I know I did way more good than bad.

With that in mind, I was/am always considering if what I'm doing is helping to get my child to a successful future. I don't want to raise an asshole. That's the goal.

In this book you will find tips to help from infancy to college. You will laugh, discover relatable scenarios, and above all . . . find grace.

Welcome to Parenthood

BABIES

*M*uch to my entire family's annoyance, I've been mothering my brother and sister since I was five years old. That, and babysitting since I was eleven, gave me great confidence that I'd be a fantastic mother. I was "experienced," people!

I had my first baby when I was twenty-six. He was the most beautiful baby ever made. I'm not just saying that because I'm his mommy. The nurses and everyone who met him would say so. I had prepared my husband and myself for an ug-oh.

"All babies look like aliens or old men when they're newborn," I told my husband. I just wanted him to not be surprised at the sure to be wrinkly, misshaped noggin of a baby that we were soon to have.

Instead, we had a baby boy with long lashes, old–soul eyes, and a precious button nose, with only a slightly misshapen noggin. His lips! Oh, my stars! This boy had ruby–red, bow–shaped lips. Gorgeous. He was super skinny, though. Usually, I don't find super–skinny babies very cute. We just didn't take a lot of naked pictures of him, but the mental image has never left me or my sister, who affectionately called him the Worm.

The Worm, darling moniker though it was, was overridden for a more suitable name. A good name. A name that will not be embarrassing when announced at graduation or when said in a wedding ceremony. A name you could add "Doctor" or "The Honorable" to. For the sake of his privacy, I'll call him Daniel.

Baby Daniel

Daniel knocked me off my mom high horse right off the bat. First, he was delivered by c-section. I really did not want it to go that way, and if my husband had been on board with it, I would've delivered him at home or at a birthing center. So already I was not the Wonder Woman I'd hoped to be.

Then the little punk gave me a challenge with breastfeeding.

I had huge breasts (past tense, as I later had a reduction) and I was finally going to use them for what they were made for, and this little baby was like, "No, thanks." Maybe it was because my boob was bigger than his head. Could you imagine how freaky that would be for a baby? I was always holding back part of my breast because it seemed like I was smothering him a little bit.

My big boobs either never produced much milk, or Daniel's lack of enthusiasm was not enough to stimulate production. I was determined to breastfeed. I mean, it's "better for baby" and . . . we were broke. No way could we afford formula. After six months of basically starving my already skinny baby, my doctor suggested I try blessed thistle and fenugreek, herbs you can buy over the counter. One fattens up the milk and the other increases production.

I gave it a try and it worked. I took it before bed one night and woke up with milk spraying out of me like one of those crazy hydro–twist sprinklers. When I pumped before the supplements, my milk looked like yellow water. After the supplements, I'd pump and my milk had a layer of fat on top. It was *magic*! Daniel fattened up in no time. Still, the child tried me.

Daniel was never diagnosed with colic, but I would guess that was it. He constantly wanted to be held and cried when he wasn't. I'd put the bouncy seat in the bathroom to set him in while I showered or pottied. He'd cry through the whole separation. There is nothing like trying to use the restroom with a screaming baby at your feet.

Sometimes holding him didn't even work. I'd go through the checklist of possible things needing attention:

- dirty diaper
- hunger
- uncomfortable garment
- sleepiness
- overstimulation

Sometimes one of those things panned out. Other times he just kept crying. Usually, I'd resort to putting him in the car and driving around. Sometimes he'd cry while I drove.

One December day when he was seven months old, he cried and cried while we drove around. "I Want a Hippopotamus for Christmas" came on the radio, and he stopped crying. You know the song? Sounds like an annoying little kid is singing it. Anyhoo . . . when the song stopped, Daniel started crying again, and so I started singing the song. I had to sing it real loud so he could hear me over his crying. I sang that song on loop for a half hour. I sang that song when it wasn't Christmas. I sang that song anytime I needed the damn crying to *stop for the love of all that's holy!*

Only one thing really helped me in those first three months. I saw a morning show interview with Dr. Harvey Karl, author of *The Happiest Baby on the Block*. He basically had this theory that babies should remain in utero for an additional three months. (How dare you, sir? How. Dare.)

His suggestion for how to soothe a baby, particularly in the first three months of life, was to essentially recreate the womb experience by implementing *the five S's*:

- Swaddle
- Side or stomach position
- Shush
- Swing
- Suck

It's genius. In utero, babies are curled up in a little ball with loud white noise, swaying as Mom moves about, and if need to, they stick that little fist in their mouths and self-soothe.

Freakin' brilliant. Does it work? *Yes.* I usually only needed to swaddle and shush, which would quiet Daniel down. I've worked the same magic with other babies as well.

Pro Tip: The shushing should be loud and close to their ear.

Bonus Pro Tip: Train your baby to sleep in any condition. That means not making the house completely quiet or dark for naps and bedtime. Toning that all down to set the mood is helpful but don't freak out with every background noise.

Let's talk about that "sleep on side or stomach" business.

Sleep (Bahahah!)

If allowing your baby to sleep in an unrecommended position is too scary for you, or if you can't lie to your pediatrician, then this is one of those instances where you should ignore my advice.

At the time Daniel was born, pediatricians recommended that babies sleep on their backs. I could not get him to sleep. Rather, I could get him to sleep, but as soon as I lay him down he burst into tears.

We had the bedtime routine: bath, book (yes, we read to our newborn), rocking then into the crib. I'd be holding my breath while I ever-so-slowly walked out of the room, down the hall, and to the couch. As soon as my butt hit the couch . . . *Waaaaaaah!*

We tried going in and soothing him. We tried letting him cry himself to sleep, but how long should you let that torture go on? (There is apparently a way to do the "crying–it–out" thing but I can't remember the rules for that game anymore. Probably since it didn't work). Finally, I put him down on his belly, and the boy slept.

I was worried the whole night but also quite relieved. If this was wrong, I didn't want to be right. At his well–baby visits the doctor would ask if Daniel was sleeping on his back, and I'd look the doctor in the eye and *lie*.

Hold on. It gets worse.

Daniel started in his crib every night. When he would wake up to nurse, I'd bring him to my bed and feed him. When he was asleep again, I'd take him back to his crib and lay him down again with the same intense care one would take while handling a live bomb. I'd tiptoe out and get back into my warm bed and then . . . *Waaaaah!*

I solved this by breaking another rule. This is not just a pediatrician rule but my own personal rule. We started co-sleeping.

I know, I know. It's a baddy. But do you know what else is bad? This woman when she has not had good sleep.

It happened innocently enough. I fell asleep while he was having that middle–of–the–night feeding. I woke up well-rested, and Daniel even slept in. I lay there looking at him sleeping next to me and I thought, "Why are we not doing this every night? It'll just be while he's breastfeeding and not sleeping through the night."

So every night we went through the bedtime routine, and I'd lay Daniel to sleep on his belly in his crib. He'd wake in the night to nurse, and I'd bring him to bed, nurse him, and *sleep*.

I remember hearing about a documentary in which mothers in other countries were shocked to learn about mothers who put their babies to sleep in "cages" (never thought of a crib that way) in a separate room from the parents. What seemed due to poverty to American mothers was actually normal and more loving than how we put our children to sleep. Their whole family slept together in one room and bed.

Note: there's good news and bad news. Bad news is the co-sleeping lasted much longer than the first year. The good news is that it did end. My kids always started in their own bed at night. They would wake up in the middle of the night and crawl out of their toddler bed and into ours for like . . . four years. They do not have sleeping issues anymore. They are not clingy and needy. It was a tough four years that I barely remember.

Bedtime

Once my kids were in a toddler bed they were going to bed without much fuss. We had a routine of a bath and teeth-brushing, followed by chase or wrestling with their dad, a story with Mom on the couch, prayers and lights out. My boys shared a room, and I could often hear them chatting with one another before they fell asleep. Once they started sleeping in their own room, Joshua (boy two), started listening to music after being tucked in. He still does this. I don't recall ever having much trouble with them getting out of bed to delay bedtime

When I was growing up, our bedtime was 8:00. I don't remember that ever changing even as we got older. At some point it did because I know I'd stay up till 1 a.m. watching TV with my boyfriend.

I have a few sweet memories as a child where I could hear the TV on in the living room. I'd get out of bed and see my dad on the couch watching *Taxi*, *Cheers*, or *M*A*S*H*. He'd invite me to join him, and I'd snuggle into my dad's side and watch late–night TV. He'd usually let me watch one episode and then would tell me I needed to go to bed. That's if I didn't fall asleep first.

We all have times when we can't sleep, and children are no different. I wouldn't punish them for it. I would suggest reading in bed, putting on some music, writing, or drawing in a journal. Give them an extra hour for one of those things and then call lights out. You may find you need to adjust their bedtime. My kids' bedtime from birth until middle school was 8:30. Middle school through high school was 9:30 on a school night. On weekends, I didn't care. Unless they had a sporting event or something the next morning, the weekend had no set bedtime.

Pro Tip: I used this with my babies and toddlers when they were obviously tired but fighting sleep. Slowly stroke the bridge of their nose with your finger. Starting up between the eyebrows and down the nose. Reflex will cause them to close their eyes and, since they are genuinely tired, they struggle to reopen their eyes. It's relaxing for them too. Do it to yourself, paying particular attention to that part right between your eyes. *Ahhhhhh!*

Trends

Everyone knows what you should do to take care of your baby. Never will you receive more unsolicited advice than when you become a parent. As a new mom I vowed to remember trends and medical advice change all the time.

For instance, I have no idea the best way for a baby to sleep now. On their side, hanging from the ceiling . . . who knows? Can they eat peanut butter or honey now? What are the new rules?

Schedules

The big trend when Daniel was born was to have baby on a schedule. I guess this works for the Type A sort of mom, so if that's you, roll with it. But for me, it really made life inflexible and the baby ruled my world. It also made me feel like the worst parent ever because I just couldn't get it to work.

Look, these little turds rule your world enough as it is. I don't know why you would want them to have any more control than they already have. Your baby does have a schedule. You'll notice they wake up around the same time every day, they eat at about the same time, they are ready for a nap around the same time . . .

Instead of forcing your baby to adhere to a specific schedule, recognize your baby has one and then live around it, not by it. Mostly it will allow you to recognize why your baby is upset while you're running that errand. Then you can both make adjustments instead of not going out because the baby does X-Y-Z at 1-2-3. Besides, their schedule is continually changing as they grow and develop. Oftentimes when your baby discovers something new or reaches a new milestone, it will affect their sleep.

Pro Tip: Avoid shopping between 2–4 p.m. It never fails that if I'm in a store at those times, there are multiple children melting down. It's either naptime or well past it.

Mommy and Me Classes

When my kids were little, Mommy and Me classes were a huge thing. I loved them. They were a great opportunity for baby to interact with others but also for *Mommy* to interact with others. If you do not attend at least one Mommy and Me class a week . . . you and your child will be absolutely fine. They certainly offer some short–term benefits, but your kid can still get into college without attending a single Mommy and Me class. I know this because I did the Mommy and Me classes with my first child but not with my second child. No one has Mommy, Me, and My Older Sibling classes.

Changing Tables and Bassinets

You'll change your baby on the floor more than on that changing table. The changer will end up being a catch-all for baby's laundry, the diaper bag, and that toy you stepped on.

The bassinet? I guess we used it for a few weeks, but a box works just as well. Seriously. You're going to spend a lot of money on a beautiful bassinet that you'll use for like three weeks.

The Nursery

The gorgeous nursery? Do it. It's so fun! If it's not ready by the time the baby arrives or you can't afford a fancy nursery, your baby will never know or care. They will still grow up and go on dates and go to school and everything else.

I Will Never

Babies don't really require "parenting" per se. Caring for a baby is about meeting their needs more than anything. Feed them, clean them, shelter them, and love them.

Throw out that list of things you said you'd never do:

- C-section
- Formula
- Disposable diapers
- Co-sleeping
- Pacifier
- Have baby toys all over the house

Whatever your list looks like, most of it's not going to make it. My sons have been unaffected by the choices we made for them as babies. Throw that list of "I will never . . . " away and take on this list of what you will do:

You Will Do Whatever it Takes.

Throughout parenting you'll need to weigh your options and choose your battles. How important is it that your kids' shirts are clean? How vital is it that your home not be littered with toys? What will happen if your child has purple hair? A lot of this stuff has a very temporary effect on your life and your child's. How you respond to things will likely be remembered and felt for much longer.

Toddlers

THE TRENCHES

*M*y favorite developmental stage is one to two years old. One-year-olds are so cool because most of the kinks of babyhood have been worked out, they can't talk so there's no sassing back, and they are discovering and learning *so* much. It's one glorious year!

This is when parenting gets *real.* Hear me now: if you bust your ass these next three or four years you will have smooth sailing the rest of your parenting career. Well . . . you'll have a less bumpy ride. It will feel relentless and long suffering, but it is *worth* it. Work hard these next few years but also . . . be chill.

Your toddler is a little scientist. Everything they see is new. They'll want to touch it and taste it. Let them. If it's not going to cause physical harm, let them do it. Let them eat dirt, let them touch the flowers, let them put the marker in their mouth and color their legs and arms (if you can't stand that, don't have markers around, but do have chalk). Let them feed themselves with their hands or utensils. Who cares as long as some of the food is getting into their mouths.

And let them fall down.

Oopsie Daisy

When I recall my childhood, I remember lots of Band-Aids and scabs. My kids hardly ever needed Band-Aids. I feel I have failed them here. We of course never want to see them get hurt, but there's a lot to learn from a fall:

- Their limitations.
- How to get back up and carry on.
- Boo-boos heal.
- You are someone to go to for comfort.

These are things that will help a person for the rest of their life. When they fall, they are learning lifelong coping skills.

The best parents I knew were sitters. Not babysitters. I mean they sat in their seats while their little one ran around and bumped into things and fell down with nothing more than an occasional "be careful" lobbed toward them.

Of course, there are times you need to get off your butt and come to the rescue, such as if they are running toward a flight of stairs or into the street. Even then keep it light and explain there was danger. "Whew, buddy! Let's not go that way. That place is for cars. You could get hurt." I even remember saying about the road, when they were older, "You could get hurt and never get up again." Too harsh?

Let them run and fall, and when they do, don't freak out. Your baby will fall and immediately look to you for how to react. I usually responded with something like, "Oopsie daisy. What happened? You fell down. You're okay. Get up. Good job! You got it!" When they fell and got hurt, I'd say something like, "Oh, honey. Owie owie owie!" I'd hug them and examine if the boo-boo needed care or not and then set them on their feet with a kiss on the head and a pat on the butt to get back out there and play.

If I freaked out though they'd burst into tears regardless of whether they were truly hurt or not.

Let Them Get Dirty

They also need to be allowed to get dirty. As I said before, a toddler is a scientist who is experimenting and learning constantly. Let them experiment. Let them taste yucky things. I usually respond with, "Ew! Blech! Let's not eat that again." More than likely they will eat it again and then repeat "blech!"

Get dirty. It'll wash off. Don't bother getting your toddler clothes they aren't allowed to get dirty in. That's just mean, really. Dirty clothes, hands, and faces are signs that a good time was had. Throw them in the tub, and while they are in there, let them splash. Again, they are learning things like cause and effect. You can always ask them to tone it down if it's getting too wet, but remember that water dries.

When the things they are doing upset you, ask yourself if it's truly causing anything or anyone harm. If not, let it be. Your child is learning about the whole world.

Pro Tip: The Italians have a word for the water/wine stain that is left on a coffee table or napkin. It's *culaccino*.

A friend told me that her father came to help her move. She had a beautiful antique armoire that her dad duct taped shut. She was so mad. When she peeled off the tape, it damaged the inlay and left a gummy residue.

Shortly after this move, her father died. Every time she walked passed the armoire she'd touch the damaged spot and whisper "thank you, Daddy." She was grateful that she had never scolded him for the damage.

We certainly want to teach our children to take care of their things and our own. Be gentle in your approach. *Culaccino* can be the impression we leave on others. It can be that water stain or it could be the way you responded to it.

You Talk a Lot

I talk a lot. I have been asked/told to stop talking since the day I learned the skill. I still talk a lot, and I talk to toddlers.

Somehow people have the impression that babies don't know what you are saying. They understand so much more than you realize. They understand your words before they can speak themselves.

One day I was visiting a friend who had a one-year-old. The little girl walked by trash on the floor. Her mom told her to pick up the trash and throw it away. I was amazed to watch this little one squat down and pick up the trash with her little dimpled hand and then toddle over to the trash can and toss it in. I never forgot it.

Once I had my own babies, I'd talk to them all the time. I'd talk about the things we saw at the grocery, about colors, about animals and the sounds they made. I asked them to help pick up their toys. Instead of constantly running interference I became a sitter, and I'd say "No. Don't touch that," from the comfort of my seat.

I also tried out baby sign language. The idea is to teach your baby some very basic sign language so that they can communicate with you when they still can't talk. It's funny that folks are so impressed by babies using sign language. No one's surprised when they wave bye-bye or blow a kiss. Those are baby signs. It does not delay their language. If anything it can expedite it. I taught my boys four signs:

- More
- All done/finished
- Please
- Thank you

That's it.

My sister always recalls the time she gave Daniel a present before he started speaking. I think it was a wooden puzzle. She gave it to him and when he opened it, he immediately turned to her and signed, "Thank you." It has been one of my greatest points of pride that my sons had basic manners before they could even speak. They still always remember to say please and thank you.

I'm also often told they have a large vocabulary. It may be because I talked to them, for the most part, like I talked to anyone else. I'd say things like, "Um . . . no, sir. That's unacceptable." I've been told that sounds pretty ridiculous, but then they'd be four or five years old and using "unacceptable" correctly. We also read to them a lot. Honestly, though, have you watched modern-day cartoons? They have a great vocabulary now, so it may be that watching TV actually had a part in it.

Joshua (Boy 2)

Joshua. This was the child that really humbled me.

While Daniel was a difficult infant, he was an easy and darling toddler. It fooled me into thinking maybe I was good at this after all. So we had another.

God gifted us with another boy. Joshua was a cutie. He was roly poly and had all the right chunky bits. We took lots of nudies of this snuggle-buggle. He was such a good baby. Nursed like a champ and joined in the co-sleeping.

Joshua was sooooo much easier as a baby. Maybe it was because of the things I learned from baby Daniel. Maybe it was his personality. I don't know and I didn't care. He was a joy.

Then he turned one.

I don't know if I was tired or depressed or both, but I was not on the ball as a mommy. I was throwing out stern "Nos" all over the place. Joshua was a super–sensitive little guy and was crushed when scolded.

One time, he was reaching for an electrical outlet and his uncle gave a firm "No." Joshua burst into tears of embarrassment. It was a different cry. He was sort of gasping between sobs. He cried so hard that he vomited, which then caused a bloody nose.

Dude! What? This kid!

My husband said, "We'll have to beat that out of him."

Now calm down. We did not beat our kids. We grew up during the era when parents spanked their children and said stupid stuff like "cruising for a bruising."

I laughed at my husband and reminded him that being sensitive is not a bad thing. This is a part of the personality he was born with. Our greatest assets can be our greatest foibles so, as a parent, I want to find the positive side of being sensitive and teach my child to recognize that. I told my husband, "We just need to teach him how to not be overly sensitive internally but to still be sensitive to others. He needs to learn to use his powers for good and not evil."

Your strong–willed child will not be one easily swayed by peer pressure. Your shy child will keep good boundaries and is probably a good listener. Find the positive in their traits and nurture that part.

The biggest compliment I get regarding Joshua is how incredibly empathetic he is. Thank God we didn't try to "toughen" him up or shame him for being sensitive.

Joshua's sensitivity was not what broke me as a parent though.

Note: At this time my brother-in-law, a marine, was on leave from a tour in Iraq. The day before he left us he said, "I gotta tell ya, I think your job may be harder than mine." I seriously doubt that, but he definitely recognized the alligator-wrestling that parenting can be when your kids are this age.

Bad Moms

My kids like to ask which one of them is my favorite. I always tell them it's the dog.

I want you to know, right now, that you will have a favorite and it will probably change from time to time. You are not always going to like your kids. Whichever one is in the Ask a Lot of Questions phase is not going to be your favorite. When they started middle school . . . gross . . . I did not like them. There is so much about middle-schoolers that I don't enjoy. I could write a whole chapter on it. My sons were two of the truly awkward middle schoolers, and I was always surprised when they came home and no one had beaten them up. I know other mothers who love middle schoolers, God bless 'em. That was just not a good time for me. Obviously, I did not enjoy age three very much either. There are lots of other times though when your child is a treasure. Just know it's okay when you are not liking them, so long as you keep loving them.

I tried to embarrass my kids. When they were in high school, I'd drop them off at the front of the school and shout, "I love you!" as they left. My sons just turned around, shouted it back, and blew me a kiss completely unscathed. Even in high school.

If I dropped off their friends', I'd shout, "I love you" to those kids too and included their names so they couldn't pretend it wasn't directed at them. They were embarrassed but you could also tell they liked it. They felt the love. My friend, Caren, would make all the kids hug her when she dropped them off. These are things that usually embarrass other kids but mine are proud to show affection and seem to think having a loving family is nothing to be ashamed of. Weird.

Bad Mom Bonus: I have always heard parents talk about how badly their children are embarrassed by them. Sometimes, your children embarrass you. For some reason, my children would run without moving their arms. I'd pull in the carpool circle and pull my hat down farther when these robotic nerd boys ran to my car. This was, like, last year.

Bad Mom Confession

I will never forget the time I thought about hurting my child.

Joshua was an infant and Daniel was two. I was potty training Daniel (or liked to think I was) and he was wearing Pull-ups. We were in the process of selling our house, so I was having to keep it clean to show as well as be ready to leave if the realtor called to show it. This was such a time.

I was changing Joshua's poopy diaper and dress him before we headed out. I could feel Daniel was doing something behind me. While wrestling Joshua into his clothes I twisted my body around to see what Daniel was doing. Daniel, my darling Daniel, had pulled off his Pull-up and pooped on our frieze carpet. If you're not familiar, frieze has long pile fibers like a modern version of shag.

I remember I shouted. I don't remember what I shouted, but I like to think it was "NOOOO" and not an expletive. Whatever I shouted startled Daniel into tears, and he plopped down on his butt.

On top of the poop.

The poop on the frieze carpet.

Right then an image flashed into my mind of me rubbing Daniel's nose in his poop like you do to a dog. It frightened me. Where the hell did that idea come from? The good news is that it got me to calm down a bit. I finished dressing Joshua while telling Daniel it would be okay. Then I cleaned up and dressed Daniel and did my best to get the smooshed poop out of my carpet before the realtor got there to show the house.

This happened another time. I can't remember which child it was or what they did that angered me but an urge to slam their head into the wall just passed through me.

Why am I telling you these awful thoughts I had about harming my children? Because I have no doubt that I'm not the only mom who has had these thoughts. We are not bad moms because we thought about it. We are good moms because we didn't *do* it.

So many new moms will be overwhelmed and drowning, and well-meaning people tell them, "You're going to miss these years." It's not really helpful to hear that when you have baby poop, breast milk, spit-up, pee, snot, and your own tears on your shirt. You will probably miss some of this time, but it's okay if you don't. It seems like it will never end, but it will.

We are not bad moms and dads when we don't like our kids. We are overwhelmed moms and dads. *Okay?* These are the times when you need to call your person, whoever it is that makes you laugh at yourself. These are the times you join an exercise program or go for a long walk, even if it means loading up a tandem stroller with the kids. These are the evenings when you open a bottle of wine and have a glass or two or three. It's okay. You're okay.

Everyone Poops

Let's talk about potty training. Oy.

My mother-in-law potty trained both her sons by the age of two. She said she started talking about using the potty when they were about twenty-one months old. Things like, "When you turn two you're going to use the big boy potty." Then when they turned two they got their big boy undies and she kept M&Ms nearby. Several times throughout the day she'd ask if they needed to go potty or she'd put them on the potty to try to go. When they'd go, they were rewarded with an M&M.

My mother said she just gave me "pretty panties" and that was that. Two-year-old me didn't want to get them dirty and so I used the potty.

Two was the magic age. I was gonna make this happen. It would especially be great for Daniel to be potty trained because I planned to have another baby soon.

I tried my MIL's strategy and started talking about the potty and letting him watch us go potty. We read fun children's books about going potty such as *Potty Time* by Guido Van Genechten and *Everyone Poops* by Taro Gomi. He was into Thomas the Tank Engine at the time and so we got cool Thomas, Percy, and Henry undies. He turned two and we reviewed the plan.

"You are gonna poop and pee in the potty now. Let me know when you need to go so you don't get your train undies dirty. If you go in the potty, you'll get a treat!"

Long story short: We ruined all the train undies.

I tried a chart that led to a greater prize at the end besides a handful of M&Ms. Didn't work.

He could make it to the potty to pee but kept pooping in his pants. This seemed to me like he knew what to do but just wasn't doing it. So I tried punishing him when he went in his pants. Didn't work.

Then I thought maybe he's pooping in his pants for attention. So I tried rewarding him by chasing him around the house and covering him with kisses when he pooped in the potty but if he went in his pants we didn't discuss it. I just quietly changed him and gave as little attention as possible to accidents.

I potty trained my son for over a year. Finally, when he was just a little more than three, he got it. It was like a switch flipped and he just got it.

Joshua demoralized me as a mother when the time came for him to be potty trained. I had also read it's not unusual for boys to not be developmentally ready to poop in the potty until closer to the age of three. So as we approached his second birthday, I did not even talk about it. He saw his brother use the potty and we read all the same funny potty books. I think at one point he asked for underwear, and we got them but . . . eh. For the most part, I just didn't work on it with him. When Daniel went potty, I'd ask Joshua if he'd like to, and sometimes he did and sometimes he didn't.

A few months before turning three, Joshua got it. Like with Daniel, a switch flipped, and he just got it. It was on a road trip with my mom. Every stop we made he used the potty. He made it on a sixteen-hour car drive with no accidents. He kept it up the whole visit as well as on the drive home. Once we got home, he flipped the switch off and quit using the potty.

I heard or read (who knows?) that sometimes kids will digress after learning a new skill, but not to worry because they'll return to it. Sure enough he did but not until he was nearly three and a half years old.

Something else changed once he started using the potty. His attitude! I'm telling you, it's somehow connected. The same thing happened with Daniel. Potty training and that rotten behavior are somehow related. It's either something developmental that has to happen or it's a personal frustration with trying to change one behavior that makes the other behavior bad. I don't know. I don't care. I just recommend not actually potty training. Period.

It's my understanding that girls potty train easier and earlier. They are most often the ones trained by age two. I'm still leery of parents who say their child was trained by age two because what I observe is it's not so much that their child is trained but that the parent is trained to get their kid to the potty in time by constantly asking and reminding their child about the potty.

I am not saying children can't be potty trained by this age. I'm just saying, why? You can look out onto a school playground and have no clue who was potty trained by age two, three, or even age four.

I know a mom whose poor son didn't master it until age four. This is more common than you know. You don't hear about it because the mom with a four-year-old still trying to use the potty is dying while the other moms say their children were trained by age two. Not all kids are the same. Remember that and be gracious and encouraging to one another.

It'll happen. Talk about it, read about it, but don't worry about it or pressure your kid to have it happen by a certain time. I promise you that, unless there's a medical condition, your child will not go to school in diapers. My mom used to say, "They'll be potty trained by their first date." A low bar, yes, but correct.

Discipline

"RESPECT MY AUTHORITY!" - CARTMAN IN SOUTH PARK

I was raised to respect authority. What that looked like was quick obedience without questioning. I believe my parents were parenting in the way their friends parented and with some of how they were parented. Adults and children were not of the same level.

Lots of my friends had rules similar to mine. Our parents decided how we'd wear our hair and how we dressed. They dictated bedtime and wake–up time. We of course had chores and our grades needed to be good. This resulted in a variety of responses between my friends and I, most not so good.

Even though I was well behaved, it wasn't until I left home that I really started to think for myself. It was little things like buying the shampoo brand I had always wanted to try, sleeping in, and figuring out my own sense of style. Because of this, it was important for me to raise kids who could think for themselves *and* be respectful.

One of my friends has a daughter who would go to school looking homeless. Her hair would be tangled or oddly styled, she'd wear a floral dress with a t-shirt over it and maybe some paisley leggings underneath and then sandals. White sandals, mind you, *after* Labor Day. My southern sensibilities were rocked. This both fascinated and frustrated me. I'd see my friend try to help do her daughter's hair, but her daughter would brush her off and tell her this was how she liked it.

What the what?

Growing up, my mom styled my hair every morning. It was a painful process as she brushed out the tangles and then put my hair into the tightest braids ever, tied up by bows that matched every color I was wearing. I looked like a doll. Absolutely precious. I hated most of my clothes and suffered from headaches due to how tight my braids were. (Mom, it's okay. It was the eighties. It was the way.)

To hear this little girl tell her mom her hair and clothing preferences seemed disrespectful and spoiled to me. Her mom wasn't in love with how her daughter looked but she'd just laugh at this little bag lady that was hers. She too grew up like me where you wore your hair the way your parents preferred and you dressed for school as if you dressed for work, or church, or a doctor's appointment, or travel . . . haha!

This same little bag lady is now a beautiful young woman who takes care of her hair and has a fantastic sense of style. She is not nineteen and just figuring this out. She arrived at this around eighth grade and has continued to develop it as she matures.

Pro Tip: After their evening bath, I'd let my sons dress in the clothes they'd wear to school the next day. That's right. If my kids looked like they had just rolled out of bed it's because they did. This was a huge time saver when getting ready in the morning. Shocking, I know.

I wish I had said no less. This may sound odd, but my dog's trainer doesn't say no. Instead, she says, "Uh-oh." I'm currently babysitting an eighteen–month–old boy we'll call Joe. My approach with him has not been too different from what I've written above except that instead of no I say, "Uh-oh! No, thank you."

I have a glass bar full of cocktail glasses in my house, and Joe's parents were shocked.

"How do you have that here with Joe around?" they asked.

"I just say, 'Uh-oh. No, thank you,' whenever he looks like he might touch it."

Seriously. That's it. He moves on to other things that he can touch and play with. Part of this is Joe's personality. Part of it is that "uh-oh" just makes the whole thing less of a big deal and so less interesting. Nothing wrong with telling your kids no. I'm not saying that's a problem. I'm saying "uh-oh" is more of a reminder and leaves it open for your child to make a choice.

When our kids started going to school we put them on the bus with a hug and a "Make good choices." Making good choices takes practice. Practicing this skill starts very early.

Joe was playing with his baby doll the other day. He was taking his toy saw and trying to cut the doll in half and using the toy screwdriver to dig out the doll's eyes. His parents are expecting another baby and the dark and twisty side of me took a video of Joe's idea of child care to send to his parents.

While I was recording Joe took a pen and opened up a coffee table book and tried to write in it.

"Joe! Uh-oh! No, thank you. That's not a book for coloring." I kept recording as Joe thumbed a few pages of the book, pen still in hand. You could see his little wheels turning as he tried to decide what the best thing to do here was. He then closed the book and returned to stabbing his doll.

"Thank you, Joe. Good choice!"

I sent the video to his parents and his mom later texted me.

"I loved how you gave him time to follow your request instead of rushing in and escalating things. It took him a minute to put the book away, but he ultimately complied without a fuss. I can easily see a lot of parents (including myself) making the mistake of taking the pen away from him and causing a tantrum instead of giving him time to cooperate. Also, it's not a sign that your child is a budding psychopath if they regularly try to saw their baby in half and "fix" their eyes with a screwdriver, right?"

She's right. It's okay. Maybe Joe will be a surgeon . . .

The point is, Joe is already getting to practice making good choices. Of course we have to choose our battles. If he had something in his hand that could hurt him, I'd make the choice for him and take it away. As parents, we're making choices too. Is this a time to give an "uh-oh" or a stern "no," because "no" is good too. It's way better than letting your child do whatever they want.

"No" is definitive. If you say no you need to mean it. "No means no" is not just in regard to sexual assault, though I think making it clear from the beginning helps in driving that lesson home. "No" does not mean "maybe" or "no after I count to three" or "talk me into it" or anything else. When you tell your child no, that needs to be it. End of discussion.

The other day, Joe was being feisty. He went over to the glass bar and acted like he was going to touch a glass.

"Uh-oh! No, thank you," I warned. He looked at me with a dare in his eyes, and he touched the glass. This warranted a change in my tone and an end to the warning.

"Joe! No."

He continued to touch it and I got up and moved him to the couch and said, "No means no. You do not touch the glass." He never went back to it the rest of the day.

Joshua Part 2

When Joshua was eight months old we moved to Missouri. I met a neighbor, Amy, who had an in–home day care. Amy had three kids of her own under the age of five and babysat an additional three or four children. She's a former teacher with early childhood education. Boy, did I luck out! I scored a surefire playdate for my kids, plus adult interaction with an adult I liked, *and* a little early childhood education myself.

One day Joshua kept reaching for decorations on Amy's coffee table. I just sat there saying, "No, don't touch. No, don't touch. No, don't touch."

I know what you're thinking. "Michal, didn't you tell us to sit and say no and that would work?" I did. If you say no and the child does what you say, then no further action is needed. If they ignore you and do it anyway then there has to be a consequence.

After the hundredth "No, don't do that" Amy stepped in. She put her hand on top of Joshua's hand and gave a firm "No." When he did it *again,* she picked him up and sat him in the Time Out Chair. She told him he could not touch her decorations and since he couldn't obey he had to sit out. I'm pretty sure he tried to leave, and Amy had me sit with him with my hands on his lap. Then she lectured me, as a good friend does, explaining how there has to be follow up. There has to be a consequence or it's just empty words.

Honestly, it's not that I didn't know this, it's that I was so tired, and I was depressed from moving to a new state. Side note: did you know that when you move it takes two to three years to settle? That means you may feel anxious or displaced for a while after you move. This will come up again later for my family.

Here's another example of Joshua's behavior:

This was before I read Dr. Leman's book *Making Children Mind Without Losing Yours* and probably the final straw before I got the book. We had lived in Missouri for only two years and then moved back to Texas. Joshua was almost three at the time and I can't recall the incident that set things off but he did something that required discipline. I am not sure anymore but I think I spanked him and I'm pretty sure it pissed him off and he hauled off and hit me. Furious, I picked him up and took him to his room. Fabulous mother that I was, I spanked him again and then ordered him to stay in his room for a time out. (That's right, I gave a lesson in not hitting by then hitting his butt).

Joshua didn't give a shiz. He walked right out of his room.

The problem with Joshua is that he's too much like his mama. We're fighters and we are tenacious. Joshua was about to learn just how tenacious I was.

I picked him up and put him back in his room and closed the door. He opened it. I closed it and then held it shut so he couldn't come out.

It was "the most wonderful time of the year" and my sons had a mini Christmas Tree in their room. I started hearing little crashes up against the door. It took me a minute to realize that the little turd was throwing Christmas ornaments against the door (the following year we only had plush ornaments on their tree.)

Once I realized what was happening, I swung open the door. Joshua tried to run past me down the hall, but I caught him. He was kicking and screaming when I pulled him down to the floor. My mother was a former special ed teacher, and she taught me a restraint they use when a child is upset. It keeps both the child and the teacher safe. Basically the child's back is to your chest and you sit pretzel style over their legs and then loop your arms through their arms allowing said child to thrash about without hurting themselves or others.

"Or others." Yeah, right. I forgot that I should turn my head the other way and Joshua slammed his head back into my nose. I'm short so his head was pretty much at the same level. I lifted my head as high as I could and looked to the side. I kept telling him that I'll let him go when he calmed down. It was like riding a bucking bronco. I could not believe how strong he was.

Worn out, he finally stopped. I don't recall the subsequent conversation but I'm certain "Wait until your father comes home" was spat out.

I felt like I'd been in a car accident. I was shaking and sore. When my husband got home I burst into tears and asked, "What'll I do? He'll be bigger than me by the time he's in fourth grade and then what?"

My husband took it from there, but I knew I had to find another way to discipline this child. Spankings pissed him off. One time I spanked him and he turned around laughing and said, "That didn't hurt." That mocking little . . .

I was again depressed from another move and from not being the amazing mother I had always believed I'd be. I went to visit an old friend, Janice.

Janice was older than me and had eleven children. You read that right. She birthed them all and many were home births. Janice was a sitter. She had to be when she was breastfeeding one baby while the other kids were running around. Janice was the best source for parenting advice because she knew what worked nine times out of ten . . . for real. We sat on her patio sipping sun tea while I told her about my struggles as a mother.

"I'm embarrassed to even tell you this when you have eleven kids and I can't even handle two," I confessed.

"Hold on one second," she said. Then she ran into the house and yelled up the stairs, "Son, that sounds great!"

"Sorry," she said upon return, "I could hear my son practicing drums and I couldn't let it go unnoticed."

Seriously? I *suck*. She's breastfeeding, hosting a guest, and acknowledging another child's good work.

It was then that Janice gave me The Book. Why am I writing this book when you could just get Dr. Leman's? Because I'm more entertaining. Ha! That and it was more than his book that helped me be the parent I am.

I read the book and I thought maybe I don't have to be a Yeller. Maybe my kids won't grow up to be assholes after all!

Pro Tip: I will never forget the other thing Janice said to me that day. Her home was relatively quiet while we visited, and I found that shocking as eight of her eleven children were at home. She said to me that taking care of two toddlers was way harder than taking care of eleven kids. When you have a large family everyone pitches in and helps. This was not to encourage having more kids but to realize that I was in the thick of it. I was in the trenches of parenting.

She would also secure one hour every day to herself. What? How? Everyone went to their room for one hour. They could nap, read, or play quietly. *All of them.*

Discipline Does Not Equal Spanking

Taking care of two toddlers exasperated me, and Joshua was a fighter. I can recall him opening the fridge and taking food out of it so often I had to put a lock on it. The final straw came after I yelled at him for opening the refrigerator and he threw an egg on the floor. I spanked his little hand, which of course wounded his heart more than it caused him physical pain. I just remember a lot of mess. I was on the kitchen floor with this wailing child and raw eggs on the floor and . . . where's the other kid?

At this time we lived in another state from our family and friends and my husband traveled for work. I was literally beside myself.

I threw myself into exercise. Those who know me are likely cracking up right now because I hate, loathe, and despise exercise. However, the local gym would watch my kids for free while I worked out. The only little hiccup there: they kept calling me to the nursery in the middle of exercises because my kid was crying. So I mustered up some tears myself and said, "Please . . . please do not call me when he cries. I am alone here, and my husband travels, and I need this one hour to myself so that I'm not on the next episode of *Oprah* for drowning my baby."

I can't believe Child Protective Services wasn't called. Don't say stuff like that to people. Okay? Say something more about how this time is necessary for your mental health. Anything but what I said. However, I was never called out of a workout again, and I looked *amazing!*

One of the biggest frustrations I hear from parents is not knowing what to do when their child needs discipline. An unfortunately misinterpreted Bible verse about using a "rod of discipline" has created generations of us who were corrected by spanking. A shepherd did not use a rod to beat his sheep. A shepherd used the rod to prod and steer the sheep in the direction he wanted them to go. *That* is what we're doing as parents. That's all discipline needs to be.

Do spankings work? Yeah. They sure do. You can have a well–disciplined child with this method, but why? It teaches kids to obey out of fear. We want our children to obey out of understanding, which has a more long–term effect than fear. This is something they will carry with them into the real world.

I think once spankings became taboo a lot of parents threw up their hands where discipline was concerned, because for generations we've known nothing else. So how can we correct our kids in an effective way?

This is where *Making Your Children Mind Without Losing Yours* by Dr. Kevin Leman came into play for me. His book teaches discipline by natural consequence.

What does that look like?

When Daniel was four, he took every toy out of the toy box and closet and every book off his shelves and tossed them into the middle of the room. Why? I don't know. Where was I while this was going on? Probably cleaning raw egg off the floor. I had just read the good doctor's book and decided to give his advice a try.

The pre-book me would've yelled out in frustration, "What have you done? What did you do this for? Get over here and help me clean this up, right now! Don't cry! You made the mess, not me!" I probably would continue the lecture while I angrily threw each toy into a bin out of frustration at being inconvenienced.

This is how post-book me handled it: In a normal voice, not yelling, I said, "Oh, boy. That's a really big mess you made. Now you've got to clean it all up."

Little Daniel looked at me incredulously and said, "By myself? I'm too little."

"You weren't too little to make the mess yourself. You can do it. I know you can."

I then left him to it. He later came out exasperated and over-whelmed by such a big job. He apologized for what he did and asked me to help him clean up.

"Thank you for apologizing. I forgive you. I'm sorry you chose to make such a big mess. I know it's a tough job you made for yourself, but it's yours alone to clean up."

It took him all day. Every time he came back out, I would let him have a short break and then send him back in. When he was finished, he called me to his room. It was beautiful. I praised him and hugged him and told him how impressed I was. I could see the floor, so I excitedly told him I was gonna top off his gorgeous cleaning job by vacuuming. When I was done, he lay down in the middle of the floor and made carpet angels. He was so proud of himself and *thanked* me for "letting" him do it himself!

I was like . . . holy crap. The book worked!

What I learned that day is I don't have to yell at my kids and allow their bad behavior to ruin my day. I didn't need to spank him to get him to learn a lesson. In fact yelling, lecturing, and spanking would've only taught him that making a mess makes Mom mad.

What he learned by cleaning his mess himself was that his actions have a consequence and that he owns his behavior as well as the consequence.

I would love to say that this worked as well with Joshua as it did with Daniel but . . . no.

Pro Tip: You certainly don't want to overwhelm your little guys, but they absolutely can and should help with cleaning up. When friends come to play, the kid's room usually ends up a huge mess that your child ends up having to clean. I would ask kids to help before they left. However many years old they are is how many toys I'd ask them to pick up. It's a huge help.

Throw-Me-Under-the-Car Threes

I never really experienced the Terrible Twos. My kids were fine two-year-olds. As they neared age three, however, things got nasty. I particularly remember this with Joshua, but Daniel was troublesome at the same age. I truly believe something developmental is happening at this time because once they were potty trained, they were *much* better behaved.

Armed with the knowledge of discipline by natural consequences, I was ready to take my nearly three-year-old on. For Daniel, who was older and had a completely different personality, it was easy. He was responsive to discipline, appreciated it even, and learned from his mistakes. With Joshua it required a lot of repetition and, at times, was much more physical than I would've imagined.

A lot of times the consequences were obvious. You make a mess, then you clean it up. You don't like what I made for dinner, then you don't eat dinner. You threw your toy and it broke, you don't get a new one.

Other times I was like . . . uh . . . what do I dooooo?

There are two incidents I recall clearly. The first happened when we were visiting old family friends for lunch in their home. The adults were sitting around the table catching up and playing cards while the kids went off to play. Joshua did not want to play with the kids. He wanted to be with his mama. Mama reeeeally wanted adult time and to catch up with these old friends. Joshua kept coming over and whining and being disruptive. I encouraged him to go and play. He wouldn't do it. I tried allowing him to stay with us, but he was still being disruptive and just bratty. I gave him two choices: he could go play or he could take a nap.

"I want to stay here."

"That's not a choice. You can play by yourself or with the others, or take a nap."

Joshua continued to argue and the whole thing was disruptive, so I removed him and took him to a quiet place on the stairs for a Time Out that I had to sit and supervise because he wasn't going to stay. When the Time Out was up, I asked him what he'd chosen to do, play or take a nap. The fit began all over again. I asked our host if we could use one of their rooms. I took Joshua to the room and told him that I was sorry he chose to disrupt everyone else's time instead of choosing to play. I told him he would need to stay in the room. He could nap or play by himself, but I was not going to allow him to make everyone else's time unfun.

He lost his shiz. He cried and yelled, and I left him in the room, shut the door, and went down to join the others. After a few minutes, things quieted down in that room. A few more minutes later a sheepish Joshua scooted down the stairs on his bottom. At about halfway down he called to me through sobbing hiccups. I joined him on the stairs and held him.

Through sobs he said, "I'm (gasp) sorry (gasp). I won't (gasp) be disruptive."

I hugged him, forgave him, and offered him water. I asked what he would like to do. He still wanted to stay with me but said he would not be ugly. I said we'd give it a try but if he was ugly again, he'd have to stay in the room.

The matriarch of the family we were visiting that day was my former piano teacher. When we left she hugged me and said, "I love watching you be a mom." I wanted to cry. I think it was my first real compliment as a mother.

The other episode was when our family went out to eat. The restaurant service was slooooow. We had waited a long time for a table and then waited a long time for service at the table. My mistake was not bringing any sort of snack to hold my hungry children over. Rookie mistake. Joshua got fussy and angry, and he was getting loud about it. Other diners were looking our way. I told Joshua if he didn't get it together, we'd have to leave the table. He of course, tested this and continued to act out. I picked him up and we went to the ladies' room.

I sat him down on the changing table and asked him why we had to leave the table. He answered through angry tears. I told him I understood he was very hungry and frustrated by the wait. "Even when we feel bad," I said, "we still need to be kind and polite. When you're ready to behave we'll go back out."

He agreed he'd behave but even as we were walking back to the table he started loudly whining again. We immediately went back into the ladies' room. What's worse was that I saw our food had been brought out. Ugh! We talked again, I told him the choice was his. He claimed again that he would behave, and we went back out and ate our tepid meal.

Both of these times I was also removed from what I wanted to be doing, but it was necessary for the lesson to be taught and learned. The next time we went out to eat I just had to give a disappointed face and say, "Dude . . . do we have to go to the ladies' room again?" He'd knock it off and behave appropriately. Or not, and we'd go to the ladies' room, but that happened less and less.

I had to remove Joshua from a good time fairly often in order to get him to make a better behavior choice. It's not fun, parents. You'll miss out on Chick-fil-a or some adult interaction, but it's crucial to stick to your guns.

Pro Tip: I once heard that a child's attention span is only about two to three minutes per year of their age. A three-year-old will have about a six- to nine–minute attention span. Oh, yeah, you ask? Then why can they watch thirty–minute TV shows? Because something new is constantly happening in the program. Anyhoo, it's important to keep this in mind when setting your Time Out time. When Joshua was eighteen months old, I only put him in Time Out for two to three minutes. If I sat with him in Time Out, I did not speak to him or look at him. No attention. If they want to be mad in Time Out, let them. This is their time to get it together.

Disciplining Someone Else's Child

Babysitting someone else's child requires you to correct and discipline them, and spanking is absolutely off the table. If a little guy is reaching for something that he shouldn't, grab his hand instead of swatting it. Remove him from the situation like in the story above.

What if the parent is there? What if you are not the babysitter but a friend hanging out with a parent and their child? This is where things can get sticky. A lot of parents bristle at anyone besides them disciplining their child, however, you still have personal boundaries that should be respected.

If you are in their home, leave it to the parent. Hard as it is sometimes, that's their home and they have their own spaghetti recipe. If their child's behavior is intruding on your personal space or things, you may absolutely address it. Some kids want to climb all over an adult or hang on them. To that you can say, "No, thank you! I'm not a jungle gym." The parent should take your cue and follow up with correcting their child.

If it continues and the parent continues to ignore the behavior, you can leave politely. An explanation is not needed at that time. You might address it later, particularly if there is another invite. Same if the child is messing with something of yours like your purse or your food (just throwing that out there). Same thing. Make it clear you don't appreciate that behavior. "Excuse me. That's mine. You need to ask first before _____."

Now, if the little stinker is at *your* house, you have a little more authority. Everything above is still the first response, allowing the parent to react to the behavior you are addressing. If the parent is not following through with correction or discipline, you can physically remove a toddler from whatever it is they are getting into that you don't like. You could even land them in their parent's lap. Maybe they're jumping on your furniture. Firmly and kindly ask them not to do that. "That may be okay at your house but not in my house."

What if it's an older child and they are ignoring your requests to respect your things? Obviously, you're not going to pick up an eight-year-old and move them to the couch. If firm requests for a changed behavior is ignored by the child and the parent, you could try saying, "Okay. Nope. We don't do that in my house. I think you need to go talk privately with your parent about this." This signals your friend to step in.

When we first moved to Colorado, we would have a weekly pizza night with our friends. This gave us all one night a week where we didn't cook, and we could all catch up with one another. One of the kids was being very disrespectful to their parents. I could see the parents were hurt and embarrassed but when addressed, their child laughed or responded in another disrespectful way. One night this was going on and I said, "No. You will not talk that way to your mother. Maybe she doesn't mind you being disrespectful to her, but I do. She is my friend and in my house. I wouldn't let you talk to any of my friends that way, let alone your parents."

I doubt this changed how they treated their parents at home but in my house, they were respectful. I mention this again later, but children appreciate knowing where the lines are drawn. They like boundaries. They really do. The kid in the above story has always been respectful to me and likes me, and has now grown up and we enjoy one another's company even more!

One . . . Two . . . Two and a Half . . .

Counting. Don't do this. I feel like it's been said over and over, but this counting business is not teaching your child anything except that they don't have to take you seriously until you get to three.

A friend and I talked about this once and he said, "So you expect your kids to just do what you tell them to immediately?"

Yes. That's exactly what I expect, and if they don't then there is an immediate consequence, not a consequence when I get to three.

I was at the pool one day and this lady was ready to go. She called for her kids to exit the pool. No one got out. So she started to count. One or two got out as she began the counting but one of her kids ignored her.

"Two and a haaaalf . . . I'm almost to three! Do you hear me?"

I wanted to push her into the pool. Come on, lady. Her children did not respect her and, frankly, neither did I. This was probably how Amy felt when I kept telling Joshua not to touch her decorations but did nothing about it.

Counting is dumb because it:

- Is ineffective in an emergency
- Displays a lack of respect for you
- Is not how the real world works
- Is a time waster
- Is annoying

Pro Tip: How often are we at the store and hear some kid wailing and angry crying? Everyone cringes. Nobody likes it, least of all the parent of the child. The parent is embarrassed. It looks like they can't control their kid. I hope to give you a different perspective on that.

The sound of an angry child should be music to every person's ears, because that's the sound of a child who is not getting their way. This child is probably experiencing disappointment. They've been told no or they've been told they have to wait. Any of those scenarios is causing the child to grow and mature, which is a benefit to society as a whole. If you see the mom, encourage her to stick to her guns or tell her she's doing a good job. A smile and a wink will do. It's just nice to alleviate that feeling that everyone in the store wishes you'd go away.

When it was my kid, I used to say loud enough for the annoyed onlookers to hear something like, "Sorry, kiddo. No means no. These lessons are hard to learn."

No Means No

The other day I was tickling little Joe. He doesn't have many words, but at one point he laughed and said, "No! Stop!" I immediately stopped. I think it's super important to respect a child's no as well as for a child to respect your no. I shouldn't need to spell this out, but your child needs to know that when someone is touching them it should stop when they request it, or you are setting them up to accept unwanted touching.

Likewise, when you tell your child to eat dinner and they say, "No," respect that. Don't make them eat.

Their no should hold as much value as your "no."

Obviously, this doesn't pertain to bratty behavior. If you tell them to do something and they say, "No," you let them know that it's not a question and they need to obey. However, make sure you give a direction and don't ask.

"Please pick that up" is a direction. "Would you pick that up, please?" is an option. I personally like the sound of asking better and tend to do that a lot. My teens will say, "Well, if I didn't have a choice, why did you ask me?" (Why you little . . . !). I then respond with, "Fine. I'm not asking. Take out the trash."

Why should they obey, though? Why should our children do what we say?

Because I Said So

How often have we said or heard "Because I said so"? That statement is asking for unquestioned obedience. Could you imagine if your boss said that to you? This isn't the military. I'm sorry but that's not enough reason to do something, and clarification is basic respect that all humans deserve, not just adults. That doesn't mean your child has to agree with your answer, it just means that you should give them one.

"Why not?"

"Honestly, sweetie, I'm just tired today and need some quiet."

"How come?"

"Because I think it's best for now."

"Why me?"

"Because I need your help."

I often used "I'm overwhelmed and can't give you a good answer right now, but we'll talk about it later." They almost never remember to revisit the conversation.

Say please and thank you to your children, because they are *people* and deserve the same courtesy you give to adults. The way you speak to them is how they will speak to you.

My smartass teen has taken to saying, "Why thank me? You told me to take out the trash. It's not like I had a choice."

"Well, you did have a choice and I appreciate that you made the right one," I'll say with a "don't try me" face.

This morning I drove that same smartass to school, and he said, "Thanks for taking me to school, Mom." I wanted to use his line that "It's not like I had a choice" but instead I said, "You're welcome. Thanks for saying it. Feels good to know you appreciate what I do for you."

Model respect for your child. Show them what it looks like and give them the words to convey it.

Questioning Authority

Questioning authority was something I never felt allowed to do. Whether on purpose or not, it was an impertinent option. No matter what parenting tools you have you will still make mistakes. When I would question my father, it was usually met with "You need to honor and respect me" or "how dare you judge me?" Maybe it was because questioning wasn't allowed or maybe it was because I did not know how to respectfully approach a person of authority.

Your child may say, "You are so mean! You think I'm stupid and can't do anything!"

Your kneejerk response to that may be to send them to their room or argue that that's not true. Maybe it's to say, "Oh, stop. That's not what I meant at all. You're being overly sensitive."

It would be better to teach your child an appropriate way to address you (and anyone, really) when they are offended. That sounds more like: "Mom, can I talk to you about something you did/said?" Then we'd find a time and place where we could speak privately. "Mom, it really hurt my feelings when you said _____. It made me feel like you think I'm stupid and can't do anything right."

My response would be, "Oh, honey, I am so sorry. That was not my intention and not what I think at all, but I see how it made you feel that way and I apologize. Please forgive me."

Then, with forgiveness and grace between us, we could talk further about the situation that brought us to the hurt feelings to begin with.

Apologize and Forgive

Having my parents or any adult in my life apologize was rare for me. I don't think my parents were jerks. I think it was just a thing adults did not do for children.

It is always crushing to hear that I disappointed or hurt my child, and it has been easy for me to apologize. However, when they'd say, "I forgive you," a part of me is like . . . "Oh ho! Do you? You forgive *me*? How gracious." It's been humbling. I want to hear, "It's okay, mom. I understand."

Apologizing isn't about getting understanding but about getting forgiveness, and the forgiveness is not so much for the violator as it is for the violated. That is more important for my children to learn than for me to preserve my ego.

Besides, that's what I've taught them to say. When one

brother wronged the other, Daniel would apologize and Joshua would say, "That's okay, brother." I reminded him that it's not okay. If it was okay, there would be no need to apologize. The appropriate response to an apology is "I forgive you," even if you don't feel it. Saying it begins to release the hurt.

Likewise, I do the same for my children. "I forgive you" is all that needs to be said. We don't need to follow it with a lecture: "I forgive you. Next time . . . *berate berate berate*." If you feel your child doesn't fully understand what they are apologizing for, receive their apology, sealed with forgiveness, and talk to them further about it another time.

At Home

EATING AND OTHER MESSES

*M*cDonalds was on my "I will never" list. I was never going to take my kids to McDonalds or Chuck E. Cheese. I'm happy to say they have *rarely* experienced either, but they have certainly been to both and more than once. Again, I advise relaxing your expectations a bit. Be flexible. Do what's best for you and your family.

The food suggestions start out the gate. It starts while you're pregnant and you're being told by Aunt Francis to be careful to not swallow a watermelon seed or it will grow inside you . . . or something like that. No seafood, yes seafood. No alcohol, some alcohol. Yes pickles and ice cream, no pickles and ice cream.

"Breast is best" is in all the books and magazines. Your friends say it, the doctor and the pediatrician say it. It makes sense. I mean . . . you got boobies, and they make milk. It should be the most natural, commonsense thing ever. As you've already read, for me it was not so natural and easy. My tenacity and stubbornness kept me at it. I was going to nurse for a year, as God is my witness.

Both of my sons stopped at ten months. Just quit. I was so

bummed, particularly after working so hard to make it work with my firstborn. I had another friend who was pregnant at the same time as me (both times, actually) and she was the fountain of breast milk. She could've nursed her babies and mine.

According to Lansinoh and the other makers of breastfeeding products, one of the benefits of breastfeeding is a reduced risk for ear infections. The Fountain of Breast Milk and I used to have a chuckle about that one as her poor babies had chronic ear infections and had to have tubes put in their ears.

I'm not saying the benefits aren't real, but I am saying it's not some magic elixir that will protect your baby from diabetes, obesity, ear infections, allergies, and stupidity. Yes, did you not know? Breastfed babies are on a path to optimal brain development and tend to score slightly higher on cognitive development tests.

Not all moms are able to breastfeed for a variety of reasons, and some moms may just not want to do it. Clutch your pearls all you want but it's really just no one's business. Formula–fed babies are not going to be knuckle draggers with severe peanut allergies. Again, you will see all the kids playing together on the school playground and have no clue who was breastfed and who wasn't. I mean . . . at least for the most part.

Chicky Nuggies

When our kids start to take solid foods there is a smorgasbord of dos and don'ts. I'm of the opinion that your child should simply eat what you eat. I used to make my kids a different meal from my husband and I. It was usually chicken nuggets shaped like dinosaurs with a side of some sort of veggie. In hindsight . . . not the best. I've seen toddlers who eat all sorts of interesting and healthy foods because their wise parents presented them with these choices.

Just tonight, the little guy I babysit, Joe, helped me make

dinner. He tasted and loved raw sweet peppers. That's something I would never have thought to offer to my eighteen-month-old. His mom always sends what was probably the previous night's dinner. Things like chili beans, spaghetti, and some sort of Asian fusion with tofu.

What if you have a picky eater? I think that's all the more reason to continue to offer a variety of foods. Pediatricians will all tell you that your child *will* eat when they are hungry and it's true. Joe is hit and miss with eating. Sometimes he won't eat any lunch but is ready to eat around 2:00 or 3:00 in the afternoon.

It's also good to remember that a toddler's stomach is the size of their fist so don't be surprised if they don't eat a whole lot. It's okay, and pressuring them to eat more after they decide they are full could create bad eating habits. If they say they are full, believe them and don't be surprised if they need a snack later.

I've seen mealtime become such a point of contention with families. It should be an easy time together as a family. If your child doesn't like what you made for dinner, don't argue with them about it or try to make them eat it. Just tell them they don't have to eat it. You might still require that they stay at the table for time with the family but they don't have to eat the dinner you prepared. They just won't eat. If they ask for something else the answer is "no." You worked hard to prepare the meal before them and that's what they can eat. You're not a short–order cook making individual meals for everyone.

None of this needs to be a fight. It's a matter of fact. If they are upset that they don't have dinner you remind them this was their choice.

"I'm sorry you chose not to eat the dinner I made. I'm sorry you chose to be hungry tonight."

You are not doing this to your child. Your child is choosing this for themselves. If they are hungry enough they will eat it. If they are stubborn enough to go to bed hungry, they'll remember the lesson. If they decide later in the evening that they would like the dinner you made, let them have it.

I recently saw an Instagram post where a parent sent their child to bed hungry and at 4:30 in the morning the child woke them up announcing they were hungry. The parent joked how their plan had backfired on them.

I disagree. They should not have gotten up to feed their child at 4:30 a.m. Instead, they should've used this to drive the lesson home.

"I'm sure you are hungry since you chose not to eat dinner last night. I'm sorry you're hungry. Go back to bed and I'll feed you in the morning."

If it's a chronic issue, ask them to help you make the menu for the week. Remind them they are *helping* with the menu. They do not have complete control of it. You won't be eating macaroni and cheese every night.

So many moms used to tell me their child will only eat such and such. "Really? Because they ate _____ at my house and loved it." They usually want to know the recipe and it's never anything special. I'm not a great cook. It's simply that the children had no other option.

Talk to your kids about food and remind them it helps them grow. It gives them energy to play, go to school, and enjoy sports. To encourage more vegetable eating, serve salad or veggies first but without the main course. Don't comment on how much they eat. Either asking to eat more or praising how much they eat can send a wrong message and create bad habits. Talk about food as fun, nutritious, and energy giving. Foods are not "good" or "bad." Serve a dessert after dinner.

A friend who struggles with her weight told me she remembers her dad being so proud of her for cleaning her plate and so she always did and still does. You can praise your picky eater for eating by saying, "I like the choice you made to nourish your body" or "I like the choice you made to feed your body and brain." This gives positive reinforcement without making it about how much they are eating and reminds them why food is good for us.

Pro Tips: A great tip my friend Caren taught me is the "no, thank you" bite. She said that if her kids didn't "like" something she served, particularly if they'd never tasted it before, she required that they take one bite before they could eschew the item.

Caren also taught me a trick of her mom's. When Caren's mom was preparing dinner she would set a bunch of fresh–cut veggies on the table and tell the kids, "Do not eat these. They're for dinner." The kids would run and play and as they'd run by the table they almost always grabbed a veggie to eat as they passed.

Also, my pediatrician encouraged us to use ranch dress-ing, cheese, and ketchup to our advantage. If it gets them to eat what's on their plate, it's a win. Condiments do not suddenly destroy the nutrition that is in the veggie or chicken that it tops. I also have puréed veggies, like yellow squash, and stirred them into their mac and cheese. They never knew.

Electronics

Never before have we had so many choices in electronic entertain-ment, and it starts very young. They say the advancement of tech-nology is going faster than we can evolve with. In other words, our electronics can do more for us and are showing us more than our brains can fully absorb and utilize.

When my eldest was born I had a flip phone that could make phone calls and take really bad pictures. The end. That's where technology was at that point. We didn't have touchscreens or apps. I think MySpace was a thing, but I wasn't on that until just before it phased out of style.

When going to a restaurant it was important to be armed with a little entertainment in your diaper bag. Our favorite was a plastic container filled with colored popsicle sticks. We'd take out the sticks, and my toddler would work on their eye–hand coordination by putting the sticks back into the container through the holes in the lid of the container. As they got older, we'd add the challenge of only putting in the sticks of a certain color.

Now, a parent just whips out the iPad and turns on a show or game for their child to play. While it certainly does the job and is amusing to see a child work their touchscreen, I'm not convinced it's the best thing for them. I think real toys and time to use their imagination are always going to be better. That said, when used in moderation, I don't think it's going to cause long–term damage to your child either.

Pediatricians recommend avoiding digital media until about age two. It's not harmful for them to sit in your lap and watch a show but having their own screen time is something to steer away from at this point. Children two to five should limit their screen time to one hour per day. Screen time before bedtime can have a negative effect on your child's sleep. Yours too, actually. It's recommended to not have screen time within that hour before bed (she said as she typed on her iPad in bed...)

When Joe first arrived at my house, the only toy he came with was a wooden hammer. I didn't have baby toys because my children were teenagers. Luckily, we had really nice weather and Joe and I would sit outside and watch the dogs play, watch the birds, and go for walks. He'd dig in the dirt with his hammer or find a stick to do the job. I've since collected a few other things to entertain him with, but his favorites are wooden tools, a crayon, and a drumstick. He also loves for me to read to him, and we play chase. We don't watch TV or play on the iPad. We don't have super–cool toys. Just simple toys and Joe's imagination. While I don't think video games are the worst things in the world, I know Joe is learning and experiencing far more than if he was on a computer.

I remember my kids always wanting a show on in the car, even if we were just running to the store. I knew a lot of parents who would allow this. For my family, the rule was no video unless we were driving somewhere farther than an hour away. What good is having it on if you can't finish the show anyway? Look outside your window, spend time with your thoughts, have a conversation or be bored. Boredom is fine too.

Phones and Social Media

When it comes to phones and social media, I say avoid both for as long as possible.

I'm going to date myself here but back in my day, if we needed to call home, we used a pay phone. Obviously, that's no longer how we operate. I can't even remember the last time I saw a pay phone. Is that even an option anymore?

At what age your child gets their first cell phone really depends on your lifestyle. It seems the young ones getting cell-phones have divorced parents. They need their phones for communicating with two different households. Some parents wait until middle school or high school. I wanted to wait until high school, but my husband got them phones when they were in middle school while I was out of town. It did prove to be helpful in communicating carpool and after–school plans.

I can understand them needing phones, but I don't see the necessity of having smartphones. Smartphones are for way more than basic communication which is really all a child needs a phone for. They're not trading stocks or checking the news. Most everything else on there is another opportunity for trouble and another issue to navigate. I'm a proponent of parental control software as you can stumble into some crazy stuff with an innocent search.

I once did a Whoville Gingerbread search for ideas for a gingerbread house I was making. Evidently . . . there are some kinky bastards who are into WhoPorn. The point is, it could've been one of my boys who googled Whoville Gingerbread and saw the whooters and buzzwinglers that I saw (How gingerbread is involved in this . . . I don't know. Also, I'm not kink-shaming. I just don't want to see it. Damn.)

As far as social media goes, I'd discourage it. It's a time waster and, again, another source of trouble. To be clear, I never felt my kids would use social media to seek trouble, but social media allows for trouble to seek them. I was very lucky in this area because my kids simply have no interest in it. Daniel only recently joined a social media site because it was the only way to communicate with his suitemates before moving to college. If they were on social media as kids, I would be on whichever one they were on and have all the passwords.

If it's even possible, I'd avoid a camera on their phones. Guys do ask girls for nudie pics and girls do send them sometimes without even being asked. And why do guys think any girl wants to see a "dick pic." I don't know a single woman who would like that or is impressed by that. No, no, no. This needs to stop.

How to avoid this? You have to talk about it. Ew. I know, but you gotta. Your child will be very uncomfortable and grossed out by the discussion to which you can say, "If you're uncomfortable talking about it, that's a very good sign that it's not something you'd want to do or see." You can also have all passwords and let your child know that you can and will randomly check their phones. Some find this to be an intrusion of a child's privacy. I see it as my phone and not theirs so . . . fair game.

Final Note: I don't have good advice on managing all the various screens. My kids play a lot of interactive video games which was a really great source of socializing for them during the COVID pandemic. We have a rule that you have to work out for an hour before you can play video games. I don't have strict phone rules because by the time they got their phones they were well behaved and trustworthy young men. They knew what was expected of them, and they never said a negative thing if I checked their phones. They had nothing to hide. When friends came over they played video games, but something switched in them around the age of fifteen. Now they would rather hang out and talk with their friends than play video games.

Privacy

My kids would run around naked after bath time, laughing and squealing while we chased them with a towel. As teens they are so prude! It is rare for them to walk around in their underwear or with a shirt off. That's not something I tried to achieve with them, it's just their preference.

Our children deserve privacy. At the same time, it is our responsibility to protect them from others and from themselves. As with bedtime and other limits we set, privacy should be an evolving situation.

When our children are toddlers, privacy isn't much needed at all. You're still helping them with dressing, bathing, and potty time. Bedroom and bathroom doors were open in those years.

My mom tells a story of when my brother was about four years old. His bedroom door was closed. When she opened the door she found him playing "You Show Me Yours and I'll Show You Mine" with the neighbor girl. From then on, Mom's rule was that the doors were only closed when changing clothes.

I don't know how Mom handled that situation but if it were me, I'd like to think I'd tell the kids that their penis and vagina are private parts that we don't share with others. I'd probably then invite them to play a board game or something in the living room. What they were doing was inappropriate, but it wasn't wrong. It wasn't sexual. They were exploring natural curiosities. I would let the girl's parents know about it and that we talked about private parts so they could follow up with their child as well.

In my house, it was my kids who sort of set the privacy boundaries. My kids kept their doors open when changing until they started bathing/showering themselves. There was no set age when we declared privacy was necessary, it just happened as they got older and started to want more privacy. When friends came to play, the door was open, but I also don't believe it was a rule of the house.

When they were teens, that changed some in that I would request the door stay open. Caren's mother-in-law told her, "I don't entertain my friends in my bedroom. The kids don't need to either." It's a funny thing to imagine your grandma in her room with her friends lounging on the furniture. It was a good point and so the pre-teens and up played in the main part of the house.

What about going through their room? Like their phone, their bedroom is mine. It's in my home. Out of respect for my kids, I don't usually go through their things but they know I can if I so choose. If your child is being secretive and/or their behavior changes, I think it's fine to investigate by talking to them and maybe even going through their room. I've probably gone through Daniel's room three times. Every search brought up boring results and confirmed that he truly was as straight and narrow as he portrayed himself. Same with his phone. I'd randomly ask for his phone and for the password and I'd rummage through it only to find boring and dorky texts and pics.

The kids did not usually lock their doors. I always knock before entering, but if I knocked and found the door locked it always made me suspicious. I'd then ask why the door was locked. I've been told, "I didn't realize that it was" or "I was changing." I'd usually respond by jokingly giving a stink eye and letting them know *I've got my eye on yoooou.*

Daniel has asked more than once why I don't trust him. "Honestly, I do. You've never given me a reason to not trust you. However, you are human which means you will make mistakes and you are ever changing. I won't be one of those parents who says, 'My child would never . . . ' The very nature of a human says that you very well could."

Joshua never closes his door except to change clothes, and he even sleeps with his door open. His room is a mess. Sometimes I wish he'd close the door so I don't have to see that mess.

Pro Tip: Today is my grandma's birthday, and she used to tell me that the kids' rooms are their domain. "Don't worry so much about if it's picked up or not," she'd say. It was one less battle for me to fight. Once in a while I'd have to insist that it's picked up enough for me to walk through and to run a vacuum but otherwise, I let it be. What real harm is it?

Sibling Relationships

I remember when Joshua was a newborn. I laid a blanket down on the floor and put him face up on the blanket. Two-year-old Daniel walked over and stood over his new baby brother and whispered to himself, "I kick it." I think I nervously laughed and removed Daniel far away from the baby.

I am a middle child. I had a big brother and a little sister. My brother and I are closer in age, but he and my sister seemed to get along with each other the most. They had the common annoyance of my constant mothering of them and tattling on them. I felt like they were mad at me a lot. There were times when we all got along really well and had a lot of fun together too.

My sons are two years apart and adore one another. They rarely argued. The bickering started around high school, I think, similarly because big brother was always correcting little brother.

I have found that's typically the biggest reason that siblings argue. I was often reminding Daniel that Joshua is not his responsibility. I was careful when they were younger to not make him his responsibility.

When the younger child comes to you whining about being bored or "brother won't play with me" it's so easy to order the older child to play with his younger sibling. In the long run it sends the wrong message to your older child. It's not their responsibility to entertain their sibling or to keep their sibling happy.

"Help your little brother with that task" is another thing I was careful of so that the younger sibling will not grow up to think it's their sibling's job to help them. I'm sure you've heard it in your own family dynamics where an adult sibling says something to the effect of "I need your help, your time, your money, your attention and because I'm family, you should give it to me." Because they're family you may be more inclined to do those things but a healthy boundary with family says that you don't have to. Family is not entitled to your help, time, money, or even your affection.

This sounds the opposite of cultivating a loving sibling relationship, but forcing our kids to do these things for their siblings creates resentment in one child and codependency in the other.

Of course they should help one another but not all the time. I tried to help my kids notice and be aware of things that need to be done and people who need to be helped. This is difficult for a young person to do, so pointing it out and demonstrating that yourself will help them develop that skill. Helping someone out of choice as opposed to being told to is very different.

Even as a parent, I did not always step in to help. It can be painful to sit and watch your child struggle with a task. It'll slow you down, but they will not learn to do it on their own if you always step in to do it for them. It's a two–for–one lesson. They learn to do it themselves and they learn they can overcome struggles.

School Days

*W*hether you choose to homeschool, private school, public school, or whatever school is a family preference. There are things I like about all of them and things I don't like about them. Just try to set aside your bias when choosing your children's education.

Private schools are not drug-free and only full of good kids. In fact it's often where the kids who have been expelled from public school are sent. Homeschooling has conveniences and flexibility but can be extremely difficult. Public school has a lot of problems but is not brainwashing children.

Finding the best school is less important than figuring out your child's learning style. Once that's discovered, it's much easier to advocate for their particular needs. Trust that the teachers do know a thing or two. They are college–educated professionals, not babysitters. Collaborate with this knowledgeable person. They know more about education than you, and you know more about your child than them.

Before we moved to Colorado Daniel was tested for the Gifted and Talented program at school. The program in Texas had the GT students in regular ed classes and then would pull them out twice a week to get more in–depth information on what they were learning in regular ed.

When we moved to Colorado, they required him to be tested again. The program here separated the gifted students from the regular ed students and worked a grade ahead of the child's regular grade level. In other words, if you were a second grader you'd be learning third–grade stuff.

Daniel was distressed from moving and leaving his friends, nervous about starting a new school, and annoyed that he had to be tested again. I acknowledged all of this and agreed that it was frustrating he had to be retested but this was how it was.

He went in to take the test angry and sad. He started the test but halfway through he pushed it away and said, "I already took this test in Texas. I want to go home. I want to go back to Texas." The observer encouraged him to try to finish the test, but he refused. I was called to come and pick him up.

When I got there, he had been convinced to finish the test. In the end he did not qualify as a gifted student in Colorado. Years later he confessed he just started answering willy-nilly so the whole thing would be over.

Daniel finished his elementary education in regular education. He had a few struggles such as being unable to finish timed math tests because instead of giving the whole number answer to 7+8 he kept thinking "7+8=10+5=6+9" and a few other hiccups. We made adjustments and he moved on to middle school. In middle school, due to standardized tests, he was relabeled gifted. He was in advanced classes as were other non-gifted kids. By high school the gifted label was completely dropped. My friend's daughter was never in GT and by high school she was in advanced classes with the same kids who had been GT in elementary school. She even made better scores than a lot of those kids.

I'm not a big fan of all of the labels because it can be more of a crutch than a badge. I understand the labels are to aid teachers and students to meet their different learning styles but it can be to the detriment of the child. The Gifted and Talented label sounds more positive than the ADHD label. A child who is GT may have some quirky behaviors that educators may be more tolerant of because the child is gifted. Likewise, they may be more tolerant of another child's behavior because they are labeled ADHD. The GT or ADHD students and their parents may also feel their behaviors should be excused because of their label. A teacher may have lower expectations of a "remedial" child as do their parents and the child themselves.

The label may be helpful for educators as they discuss certain issues, but overall I can't find a good reason for the student to be aware of the label. In the end, these kids will become adults who get jobs where they are rarely given accommodations or special adjustments according to their special label. Teach them to adjust and switch gears accordingly.

I know of many cases in which a professional said a kid would never achieve a certain level but then they did because the parent believed they could and the child never knew they couldn't.

One friend I grew up with was in a special ed class. He never made very good grades in school and was often in trouble for bad behavior in class. One year he got mad because the other students in his special ed class couldn't spell "elephant," but he could. He wanted out of special ed and requested to be retested. He scored above average and especially excelled when learning in a hands–on lab setting. Even with this discovery, he really never did well as a student and was still a behavior problem. I fear the label stuck to him and he wasn't able to break out of it until he joined the military where you learn hands on and where they don't accept excuses.

Every child is gifted. Every child is exceptional. Every child's specialness will be different. That's exactly why it's special.

Participation Ribbons

Can we not, with the participation ribbons? Besides group projects in school, this is the biggest bunch of communism ever. If your kid loses, it stinks, but it's real life and it's a learning opportunity. We have to let our kids hurt or be uncomfortable sometimes. They will get their feelings hurt, they will fall down and hurt their bodies, they will have their heart broken, they will lose people they love. We experience so much loss in life. Shouldn't some of those losses be felt and experienced in their parent's lap instead of when they are grown and on their own?

Losing teaches us we have room to improve. It gives us new goals. It teaches humility. Like falling down, it teaches us to get up and try again. It teaches reality.

The events of the past decade have implied that when you lose you should make a big stink and fuss about it. I seriously blame participation ribbons for this and for not teaching kids how to graciously accept a loss. You shake your opponent's hand and congratulate them on playing better than you. You review what went wrong and you work to strengthen your weak spots.

I did not play the sports. I did theater, not as a child but as an adult. Typically, there is one lead role. You are either cast in that role or you're not. Or you're not cast in the show at all. It's not always because you don't have the skill. Sometimes you don't look the part. Sometimes you did great but someone else simply did better. I have had parts with fifteen minutes of stage time and I have had lead roles. I've learned from every one of them.

For the love of all that is holy, please don't blow smoke up your kids' butt. Do not tell them that they are the best at something when they are not. They will be that chick on *American Idol* tryouts bawling their eyes out because the judges said she was tone deaf but her mom has always told her that she has an amazing voice. Do not embarrass your child this way. Instead of being proud that they are the best, be proud that they did their best.

I had a friend whose children were very confident. They just popped out of the womb that way. She wanted to instill some humility for fear of confidence becoming arrogance. She would tell her kids, "There is always someone better than you." It was a reminder that you will not always be the best, and that's okay. This, unfortunately, backfired with one of her kids who internalized this as "You will never be the best, and you will always be less than."

Balance is key and you don't want to make them overly confident, but you don't want their goals to seem unattainable either. Do they love it? Are they having fun? Then fan that flame by letting them know that you know they'd be a great _____ one day because they have the passion to train and work at it.

My sons have tried basketball, soccer, lacrosse, and track. They were not good at any of them. They had fun with their friends and tried their hardest. They learned how to graciously lose and to occasionally graciously win. Losing is not fun and they often wanted to quit but we reminded them that they made a commitment to play. They didn't have to play next year but they had to finish this season.

To piggyback on the value of learning to lose, I want to speak to the value of involvement in extracurricular activities. I think it's so good for a child to have something besides academics. We don't all shine in school, and shining is important to experience from time to time. It also gives you a "family" outside of your relatives. Kids in sports, theater, band, and other extracurriculars have a group of people they connect with, learn with, and experience things that they just won't have from sitting behind a school desk. They have a support group.

It also gets them out from behind their phones. They are interacting and communicating with actual people and not just texting. There's a hat for every head; there are all kinds of clubs and if your child's niche isn't there, encourage them to create the one they feel is missing. Every teenager thinks they are weird. Extracurricular activities help them to find the like–minded weirdos they can be themselves around.

Pro Tip: One way to help your child find their niche is to do like my friend Caren did. Each child needed to participate in a sport and learn to play an instrument. It meant that Caren was driving to one practice or lesson every day, but her girls were able to find something besides academics to excel in. One daughter can play just about any instrument she picks up. Another played sports throughout middle and high school. She no longer plays team sports but is still an active skier, rock climber, and hiker. The third is an aerialist, actor, and singer. My kids play video and tabletop games.[1]

Everyone's Invited

My kids would sometimes get party invitations from a classmate who they'd never talked about.

"Who is this person?"

"She's a friend from school."

"Is she a friend or an acquaintance?"

Particularly in this age of Facebook, I think it's important to teach our children the difference between a friend and an acquaintance. Being nice to everyone doesn't mean that everyone is entitled to the privileges of friendship. This is discussed more in the part about bullies. Since everyone is not your friend, everyone does not need to be invited to your birthday party, nor do you need to feel obligated to go to their party.

I love parties. I throw them all the time. Themed parties are my *life*! What I've learned though is that large parties are really not fun for a child. It's so overwhelming. I read in a parenting magazine or something to just invite one child plus one per age of the birthday kid. So when your kid is turning two, invite three kids. When they turn eight, a party of nine.

I'm not one for doing a simple party because it's what I like to do, but every party does not have to be a grand affair. The kids are just happy to get together, eat some food, and have some cake. If you do party favors, I suggest you avoid those little plastic toys and candy. It all just goes in the trash.

When my son had his Hobbit party, we gave the kids a necklace made of pleather and had a gold plastic ring on it. That was it and they were thrilled. At the camping party they all got little flashlights from the dollar store. Just don't stress about it. They are all easier to make happy than you think.

A party alternative is always cool too. Instead of a party allow them to invite one or two friends and go to a museum or the zoo or out to eat. An activity is a great gift too. I knew parents who were really good about this. The gift to the birthday kid would be a coupon for a special outing with that friend. My mom would order them a really cool decorated cake in lieu of a toy. I appreciated those gifts so much more than another toy that would clutter my child's room.

Pro Tip: I used to be so much better about this but before or after Christmas we would do a toy purge. The kids had three piles:

- Keep
- Throw away
- Give away

Each toy went into one of those piles. I tell you, we'd find things still in their original packaging. This made room for all of the new toys they got for Christmas, and it was up to them what was kept or moved out.

Let Your Freak Flag Fly

As already established, my kids are extremely nerdy. They have just always been very cerebral. From a young age they started watching documentaries. When Daniel was obsessed with trains, he'd watch documentaries on them, and we'd go to museum exhibits about trains. He could tell you all the parts of a train and the various cars and engines of trains. For both boys, history documentaries have been their favorite. We can't watch a movie without one of the boys calling out historical inaccuracies.

Very annoying.

No matter what society was going to tell them, I wanted my boys to be proud of their nerdy ways, intelligence, and unique interests. We were always pointing out what a nerd their dad is and that nerds *rule!* I honestly don't know if it's because of this strategy or because society actually does seem to be valuing nerds and dorks right now, but my kids are proud of who they are and are leaders in their friend groups.

I'll sometimes ask them, "Is that really what you want to do? Wear? Be into? It's . . . kind of strange."

They just don't care. They don't care if their other friends are into it or not. They don't care if they are the only ones not cussing or if they are the only Christians in their friend group. They don't care if their shoes are not stylish if it's the shoe they like.

How did that happen? I'm asking myself that right now. I'm not sure it was something I did on purpose. I guess it's because, if they were interested in it, I'd encourage it. If they liked the clothes, I let them wear them. As far as our faith goes, we've always shared our beliefs with them but it was never pushed on them and we have permitted questioning of their faith. We have friends of varying faiths and so they don't see it as odd or difficult to be the only Christian in their friend group.

When the boys were little, they started wearing galoshes. We called them chicken boots because our friends with chickens wore them when they went out to feed their hens. I loved it because they could pull them on and off themselves which made getting ready easy. They wore them with jeans, and they wore them with shorts. Sometimes they wore a cape as well.

Chicken boots went by the wayside when elementary school started. No specific reason. They just did. Daniel didn't have any trademark looks except maybe that he'd combine some interesting colors. When I'd say something about it he'd just shrug and sometimes ask, "Is it really that important?"

Well, no. It's not important that their clothes match. The "win" here is that they are dressed and that they dressed themselves.

Joshua was into *The Hobbit* and I threw him a Hobbit birthday party one year. Most every party we had involved dressing up. Joshua wanted to dress like Bilbo Baggins. At a thrift store, I found a woman's burgundy corduroy blazer for his costume. That blazer became his trademark. He wore it everywhere and with everything. When he grew out of it, I got him a new one. Then he started sporting other colored velvet blazers. This same kid can't match his socks and is wearing dress socks with tennis shoes and a velvet blazer.

Choosing Good Friends

Good friends will come from a variety of places. They will come from church, school, your neighborhood, and extracurricular activities. I do not like all of my sons' friends, but no one was ever off limits unless they had a negative influence on my child's behavior.

When they are toddlers and school aged, you have more control over who they choose to play with. When I saw a child whose behavior I didn't care for, I'd ask my son what he liked about this child. I may even say, "I really don't like how they talk to their parents" or "I don't like how they treat the other kids. What are your thoughts on that?" We'd be able to talk about it and we would usually add the little turd into our prayers. If the child came to my house, I'd request they follow my house rules and if they could not they would have to leave and may not be invited back.

I felt like this was a way to demonstrate to my sons how you can love someone while still requiring positive behavior and healthy boundaries.

When Daniel was in third grade, he had play dates at a friend's house. I knew the mom from volunteering at the school. She seemed very nice and was a church goer. The play dates started with me coming along and then my son would ride the bus home with her son and I would pick him up later.

One day after a play date my son said he needed to talk to me. He saw something at this boy's house, and he knew it wasn't right for kids. He saw magazines of naked women.

On the inside I was pissed! On the outside I could see my son needed comforting. He was so upset with himself and felt he had done something wrong. I assured him he did nothing wrong, that the wrong was in the accessibility of the magazines to little kids, and I was so sorry it had happened. Then I had to call this boy's mother, who was horrified and apologetic. Long story short: no more play dates at their house. They could play at a park or at my house.

Then we moved, so that was that.

Another time one of the boys was invited to a friend's house whose parents I'd never met. I asked to speak with the mom on the phone and we arranged a play date. Their home was really close by so I knew if there was any trouble I could be there quickly. I pulled up to a very small and rather unkempt home. Mom came out to meet me and was a *mess.* Terrifyingly skinny, dirty cutoffs and tank top, her eyes sunken with circles around them, her lips looked severely chapped and had red sores, and she was missing teeth. Her voice and figure were youthful but her face looked old.

It was in that second, as my son hopped out of the car and ran to greet his buddy, that I realized I had just dropped him off at a meth house. I told her I would be running a few short errands and would be back very soon to pick him up. She assured me I could take my time. Very nice lady. I then went straight to my friend's home and freaked out while she asked, "Why did you leave him there?" Long story short: He was there maybe forty-five minutes.

No harm came to him, and that family moved, so that was that.

My sons' core group of friends are good kids from good families. They are mostly from our old pizza night group. They have another circle of friends that are a little more interesting. They are the kind of kids I think my parents would have steered me away from so as to keep away any bad influences.

What about the good influence your child could be or that your family can be?

I have often overheard my son on a phone call with a buddy and saying things like, "No, dude! Don't do that! If I did something like that it would break my mom's heart." Or "Have you tried talking to your parents? Try it and maybe don't be so combative in your approach."

These more *interesting* kids come to our home and comment to the boys how nice we all are to one another. They sometimes talk to me about their problems. Even though they are not my favorite kids or who I'd really wish for my kids to be around, I am so glad we can provide a soft and safe place for them and be an example of healthy parent–child relationships. Again though, if these friendships are having a negative effect on your child's behavior, ask your child questions to help them see that maybe this isn't the best friend choice. If suggestions don't work, you may have to intervene.

Fun Note: My sons have told me several times that their friends are intimidated by me. This pleases me. Haha! One time, I overheard them playing Dungeons and Dragons and one of the kids said, "Your mom would make a great D&D character." Be still my heart!

Bullies

Both boys had a little bully trouble in middle school. I totally expected this. Actually, I'm surprised they weren't bullied more because they were kilt–wearing nerds and ran with their arms down by their sides.

One time Joshua came home upset because another child called him fat. It wasn't bullying though. They were playing make believe and this kid said, "You can be this guy because you're fat." They were in elementary school. This wasn't a mean kid. This is a kid who needed to be taught a better word to use than "fat."

I don't throw the word "bully" around lightly. Please stop saying your child has been bullied because one time that one kid called them "shorty." As a child I was teased by various people for having a "boy's" name, for being short, for wearing glasses, for a bad haircut, or for how I was dressed. It happens to everyone. What doesn't happen to everyone is to be singled out by one person or one group of people and repeatedly harassed daily by said people.

So when Daniel came to me to say he was being bullied I was like . . . mmkaaaay . . .

"Tell me what's going on."

It was mainly one turd who was giving him crap at recess. If Daniel's ball got away from him, the turd[2] would throw it far in the opposite direction or he'd peg Daniel hard with the ball. He'd kick dirt at him . . . you know, regular playground bully tactics.

We discussed strategies like trying to play in an area that was not near where this kid and his friends played, making sure a teacher was nearby to witness things, keeping his own circle of friends with him. We prayed for this turd, as he may be having hardships we didn't know about that made him act like a jerk (i.e., fostered empathy and understanding that people act out when they are hurting).

One day, I picked the carpool kids up from school and one of the kids told me that he witnessed Daniel being bullied in gym class. It was confirmed to be the same turd who had been giving him trouble. Daniel wanted to avoid the whole conversation, but his friend told me how they were playing kickball in gym class and, when the coach wasn't looking, the turd would throw rocks at my son.

"There he is," said the friend, and he pointed the child out to me just as our car passed by.

"The kid in the red hoodie?" I asked as I whipped the car around.

Daniel and his friend ducked down to the floor of the car. The young ladies in the car were stoked to see what I was going to do.

I pulled up to the hooded turd at the same time his mom did. I called out to him, "Hey! Are you the turd? I just wanted to thank you for how kind you are to your fellow classmates."

The turd turned red as he got in the car and his mother looked confused. Clearly she knew her child.

"Yes, especially at recess and in gym class. I understand you are really nice particularly at those times. Keep it up, and I'll be sure to let your teachers and principal know!"

That night Daniel said, "Our mom isn't cray-cray but she is pray-prey. First she'll pray for you and then she'll prey after you!"

Joshua's bully was not physical and was also in middle school because that's when children become particularly rotten. Joshua was friends with this guy. There was a group of four or five that had lunch together and hung out at recess. This turd was manipulative. He would make Joshua the butt of all of his off–color jokes. When Joshua would ask him not to and told him it hurt his feelings this turd would apologize and promise not to do it again.

But he always would.

Joshua made friends with a kid who was new to the school and brought him to the lunch group but this turd told Joshua not to be friends with the new kid.

I told Joshua that this was not a healthy relationship. It was classic abuse. Likely this boy was abused, or he had a parent who was and he was mimicking the behavior. There was another boy in the group who was also struggling with the way this turd was treating him. I reminded him that this turd had no authority over them. Joshua kept giving him chances and after the third time of him coming home in tears because of this turd I told my son he needed to end the relationship.

"Sit with the new kid. Make a new group of friends. See if the other kid, who doesn't like this turd's 'friendship,' wants to join you and the new kid."

Joshua was game to try but this turd wouldn't leave him alone.

"Why aren't you sitting with us anymore? I won't act like that anymore. Come sit with us again. You say you're a Christian, but you aren't acting like it." This turd was also a "Christian" and knew Joshua's faith meant a lot to him so he'd use this as a manipulation tool. This turd also went to the counselor's office and told her about his problems with Joshua and the counselor encouraged them to make up.

On it went. I told Joshua again that I did not want him being "friends" with this kid. They had classes together and he always chose Joshua to be his partner or work in his group. So I sent emails to his teachers and to the school counselor explaining the problem. "Please do not have them work together and please do not encourage this friendship. If a young woman's boyfriend was telling her who she could hang out with, hurt her, apologize and then hurt her again it would be obvious abuse. This is not a healthy relationship."

One day Joshua called me from the principal's office crying so hard he could hardly speak. Apparently, this turd tried yet again to manipulate Joshua into being "friends" again. His refusal to accept Joshua's repeated no's caused my boy to break. He left for the principal's office because he didn't want to hit this turd.

I went to the school to pick up Joshua. While I waited in the front office for him, who should descend the stairs but this turd.

"Hey, aren't you this turd? Come here a minute. Stay away from my son. Got it? You are *not* a good friend. When someone says you are hurting them, you don't keep doing it. When someone tells you they no longer want to be your friend, you need to respect that boundary. Friends don't humiliate each other. You don't make your friend the butt of all your jokes. Yeah. I've heard the jokes. You want to tell me one of them?"

Of course he didn't. Not only were they mean but they were sexual in content. Instead he said, "We all joke with each other, that way and no one else gets upset."

"Good. Then those are your people. Those kids are your friends. My son isn't. Do not apologize to him, do not work with him, don't speak to him. If you do, your parents and I will be having a meeting together with the principal. Capisce?"

Pray-prey, y'all.

I think it's good to let your kids try to handle these problems on their own, but if nothing changes, *step in*. Teach your kids to defend themselves with strategies and physical defense. They don't have to be nice all the time. Especially our young ladies. Stop teaching them that being nice is more important than being respected or safe. This is the reason Daniel was carjacked. Story to come.

The Smelly Kid

What if your kid is the smelly kid? How do you get them to keep up with hygiene? For starters, if you've read this far you already have a child that respects you and understands consequences for their actions. Maybe? Haha!

Continuing from that, hygiene can be encouraged by teaching the consequence of, for example, not brushing your teeth: You'll have to have cavities filled, your gum tissue can get disease which can cause bone loss which will eventually cause tooth loss.

There is a misconception that you don't have to take care of kids' teeth because they'll be falling out anyway. Here's why that thinking is stinking:

First of all, teaching good dental hygiene should start when that first tooth appears. Brushing those baby teeth or wiping them with a wet washcloth keeps them clear of bacteria. This not only keeps the tooth healthy but prevents bad breath. If a baby's teeth decay it can interfere with nutrition and speech development. If the bad teeth fall out early they don't hold the proper placement for future teeth which can cause the permanent teeth to come in crooked.

You should be brushing their teeth for them until about age eight. Even then, you'll want to be supervising brushing in the morning and before bed. A full set of teeth should be brushed for two minutes and be sure to brush the tongue! Like a good nerd, Daniel sets his stopwatch for two minutes, but you can make it fun by playing a song. Most children's songs are about two minutes long.

Why should they wash their hands or bathe? Germs. Germs make us sick, and bacteria can make us stinky. I used to ask my kids, "You don't want to be the smelly kid, do you?" Again, make hand-washing fun with a song and maybe some fun soap.

Bath time is fun with bubbles and toys. No one wants to do an activity that always ends up with them getting in trouble so let them have time to play, let them splash a little. Take turns with cleaning. You wash their feet and then have them wash their own feet. That way, they get practice with the task but you don't have to worry if they missed a spot.

Deodorant may need to start before middle school. Ask any teacher, your kids stink! Let them choose the scent of deodorant they like.

When Joshua was in elementary school, he took those state standardized tests. One morning he got up and was digging through the dryer to find his "lucky underwear." We found them and off to school he went. The next morning he had the exact same clothes on as the day before.

"Dude, you wore that shirt yesterday. Go put something else on."

"But this is my lucky shirt!"

"Wait a second . . . does that mean you still have on your lucky underwear?"

"Of course. I'm not taking these tests without my 'luckies'!"

I allowed it. Sorry, Ms. Davis . . .

Daniel was never hard to keep clean. He likes to do things right. I would have to inspect behind his ears every now and then but for the most part bathing, trimming nails, and dental hygiene were all tasks he took care of on his own.

Joshua though . . . he needed more reminders and motivation. He really hates the trimming–of–the–toenails thing. What worked for him may not work for all kids, but these were my tricks.

Joshua likes rituals and the finer things. He loves to steep hot tea made from loose leaves and prepared in his nice teacups. A hot shower lit by candles is always nice too. I once got him a bathrobe and slippers to encourage him to shower. I told him how great it felt to get into a robe after a hot shower. It worked.

I struggled to get him to shave. One year he was really into a certain brand of soap because the ads for it were funny. He really wanted this soap, so I ordered it because a clean teen is rare. On their website I found that they also had shaving supplies. For Christmas, I got Joshua a shaving mug, shaving soap, and the shaving cream brush. Ritual. A gentleman's tools. It worked.

For his feet I thought he'd be totally down for a pedicure, but we had a huge fight over it. He said it was emasculating to which I told him of the many men I knew who get pedicures.

"Well, Jesus didn't!" he poorly argued.

We had a good laugh as I reminded him that Jesus not only got pedicures, but he gave them as He washed all of His disciples' feet. Bam!

It did not work.

In conclusion, make sure they know why we keep clean. Give them choices in their hygiene products. Make it fun or even special. Remember that all kids stink. Even the girls. Oh, Lord, the volleyball feet . . . the long dirty fingernails . . . there's a certain group of girls who know I'm talkin' about them. They are all clean and lovely ladies now.

Great Expectations

Besides performing in theater I've also been the director of drama camps and children's performances. I've always been hesitant to take these jobs because not all parents have the standards and expectations for their children's behavior that I do. I've learned though that most kids aren't naughty because they're jerks but because they don't know what's expected of them. They just need to know what the rules and boundaries are.

One of the first children shows I co-directed starred a brilliant boy. He not only knew his lines but everyone else's as well. He knew their lines, their songs, their choreography, their entrances and exits. He knew everything. Man, it was annoying.

When it wasn't his part, he'd be whispering the other actors' lines and giving them direction. I was constantly having to remind him that that's my job, not his, and that he needed to only concern himself with his part. When he wasn't on stage, he was disruptive. He was just a lot. A lot of energy and a lot of know-it-all-ness. If someone was talking while I was talking, it was him. He made me crazy, and I was sure I made him crazy because I was always cracking a whip at him.

My co-director was the beautiful, smiling, fun one and I was the whip cracker. I was the one making them behave and teaching theater etiquette. I mean, not *just* me but . . . I was most strict about it. I was pretty sure these kids hated me.

Opening night the kids were handing out gifts and hugs and I was surprised to be a recipient. We all met in the green room to circle up for a pep talk. When it was over, the know–it–all kid threw his arms around me and gave me a huge hug. I looked at my laughing co-director in shock and discomfort. This child had been my nemesis for months and yet he loved me.

There was another show where I cast a young man in a good role but not the one he hoped for. The co-director of this show warned me he was difficult and troublesome. He was a tall kid, ready for high school, and this woman said she was sometimes afraid of him due to his size and temper. Consequently, she was afraid to tell him he didn't get the part he wanted.

She was right. He didn't like the role he'd been given and was angry and combative. He also had some pretty good acting instincts.

Since his part was small, he had a lot of downtime and so I'd ask him to be my other set of eyes. While the other kids ran through their scenes, we'd collaborate on ideas for making the scene run smoothly.

In the end, he did well on his part, and he was never a

behavior problem for me. I showed him respect and he respected me.

This has happened at drama camps as well. The kids I have to wrestle with the most tend to be the ones who end up liking me the best. The ones who other teachers have said, "he's trouble" were the ones that I was able to find a place for. When others are constantly lowering their expectations of them, I was insisting they step it up and they did. This isn't a testament to me, it's a testament to them. They were always great kids; their bar had just been set too low.

When we lived in Missouri, I would sometimes keep my neighbor's daughter. She was five years old. My kids were one and three at the time. This little girl was very smart, a goody two shoes, and kind of unfriendly to be honest. She would order me about all the time. "I'm hungry. I want lunch. I'm thirsty. I need a drink." It did not take many times of watching her until I finally sat her down to tell her she was rude. I didn't say that but . . . you know. I told her that I would appreciate her using her manners when asking me for things.

"Manners?" she asked.

"Yes. You know what manners are." I assumed she did, but the more we talked the more I realized that this little girl truly had no clue what I was talking about.

I taught her about how to politely ask for things with a "may I, please" and a "thank you." She really liked learning this and liked using manners. Every now and then she'd ask, "What am I supposed to say again?" After that we got along so much better. She no longer seemed rude and unfriendly. Now she was smart, kind, and a joy to be around.

Pro Tip: Because I'm five feet tall, kids seem to think that I'm one of them. I've been careful to keep a respectful boundary and not allow kids to be too familiar with me. I am friendly but I'm not their friend. One way that I do that is by insisting on being called Ms. Michal. I'm not Mrs. McDowell as that feels too formal and unapproachable. I'm not Michal. That's what my friends and colleagues call me. "Ms. Michal" reminds them to not joke with me like they do their buddies and to respect me as an adult even though I'm kid sized.

Another boundary hard for kids to learn is to not interrupt. I can't recall where I learned this but I taught my children that if they need/want to tell me something while I'm already talking to someone else that they just need to say "excuse me" and to place their hand on my arm. I respond to their signal by putting my hand on top of theirs so they know I'm aware they need to say something. When there is a pause in conversation, I tell the one I'm conversing with to excuse me and then I turn my attention to my child. They love having a secret signal and I love not being interrupted.

Will They Ever Shut Up?

The short answer is that most do. They'll get to an age where they retreat to their bedroom and you only see or hear from them when it's time to eat. Until that time comes the crying, the babbling, the constant questions that *never stops!* Sometimes I would just have to say, "Guys, I really need quiet right now. Please. Just stop talking until we get home" or whatever. All of this will come back at you though. Your child will say with a big sigh, "Mom, I just really need quiet right now." Friend, you better do it. Do to them what you want done to you. Right?

I read somewhere that if you listen to the little stuff, your kids will come to talk to you about the big stuff.

I knew it was true when I read it and thought, "Oh, man. Seriously?" My sons talk about the most boring things ever. They are excited about it and laughing and my eyes glaze over as their voices become muffled background sounds while I make a grocery list in my head. It made sense though and I knew I wanted them to always be able to come to me with the big problems. So I have listened about the robotechs and the pokey poos and whatever it is that they were into when they were little. I've endured lengthy discourses about various canon of various sagas. It's a painful exercise in the hopes that your child will talk to you about something of actual importance one day. I'm here to tell you, it works.

My sons have often approached me in a serious tone asking for a time when we could speak privately. My kneejerk response is to say, "Squee! *Yes!*" But you have to keep your cool so you don't scare them off. I would casually say "Sure," and we'd find time to talk. I usually drop everything and try to be chill while we walk to my room for privacy. It was in these times that they have talked to me about their fears, philosophies, and hopes. They've asked me about how their body works and about relationships both platonic and romantic, all of the things I'd always hoped they'd be able to share their thoughts about.

Besides listening to the mundane, I've created opportunities for deeper conversation. When they were little and I tucked them in at night, we'd say prayers together. Before starting, I'd ask them if there was anything specific that they wanted to pray about. It was in these times I'd find out about a friendship that may be struggling or a school project that's looming. Sometimes it was a concern that my child didn't even need to burden themselves about.

I remember one night Joshua was upset because he heard on the news that a huge "salami" had wiped out some islands. He was very afraid it could happen to us too.

"I think you mean tsunami." I explained what a tsunami was and relieved him of that fear. We prayed for those affected, and he started collecting coins to donate to aiding those displaced by the salami.

Pro Tip: As they got older and I stopped tucking them in at night, I'd use dinner time to get a glimpse into their lives. To this day we still go around the table and ask about everyone's highs and lows or best and worst parts of their day. One rule was that you couldn't say the best was "that it was over" or the worst was "school." You had to give something specific.

Tattletales, Whiners, and Cussing

While we want to be good listeners, we don't have to listen to everything.

The little girl I used to watch who had no manners was a major tattletale. It made me *crazy.* When she (or any child) would approach me with that voice indicative of tattling I would stop them and ask, "Is anyone or anything damaged?" If the answer was no then I told them they'd need to solve whatever the problem was themselves. I just couldn't stand playing referee to every seemingly bad deed.

My friend Caren pointed out it's not always that they want you to fix a problem but they just need to tell someone. When my son would approach with that tattle tone, she'd silence me with a hand on my lap.

"So-and-so said a bad word!"

"Thank you," she'd say, and the tattletale would run off.

I liked this method because it still leaves them to solve their problem, but you are able to hear what the problem is. You know, in case you really do need to intervene.

Similarly, when my kids would whine about something, I'd

shut it down by saying, "I'm sorry. I can't understand what you are saying when you talk like that." They will still say what they need to whine about but without using that high–pitched, nasally, squeaky–wheel voice. Where do kids learn this? They all do it. Seinfeld still does it.

I want to address the tattle that someone said a bad word. I would not leave your cocktail to go and address such a thing. That's one you can talk to your child about later.

When we first moved to Colorado, it was a bit of a culture shock. We moved here from Texas which has a church every quarter mile and people decorate their homes with scripture and ornate crosses. My Texas friends may not realize it's not like that in other parts of the country. I didn't realize it anyway, until we moved to Missouri and then to Colorado. Anyhoo . . . they also didn't cuss in front of children in Texas. Basically, in the south, you function under the assumption that everyone is a churchgoer.

We moved to Colorado and made friends with another family whose children were similar in age to our kids. One of our new friends sat with his daughter in his lap dropping bombs of color left and right. It shocked and amused me. Daniel piped up in the tattletale tone and said, "You said a bad word!"

I'd never really spoken to my kids about this before because I don't think anyone had ever just let it rip like that in front of my kids before. What bothered me more than the cussing was hearing my son correct an adult's behavior in their own home.

On the spot I came up with this realization: cussing is an adult's choice. My children are not allowed to cuss, but when they are adults they can if they so choose. Just like alcohol. Kids are not allowed to drink alcohol, but they may when they are adults if they choose to.

My kids never cuss. A lot of their friends do, and they have friends who give them a hard time because they don't cuss but they are unwavering in keeping this standard. It may be because their mother cusses like a sailor and so they see the tackiness of it. Either way, I did good in this area.

I really do hate hearing kids cuss though. It's not cute or funny to me. It's like when you see a child who's dressed seductively—it's just wrong. However, cussing as a whole is not a big deal to me.

In my travels I have learned that while "shit" is a pretty offensive word in America, it has about as much weight as saying "poop" in another country. "Bugger" means nothing in America but is very offensive in the UK. The word "fuck" is likely arrived from Dutch roots and means "to strike" and not "to fornicate." Words evolved over time and have been given new definitions and new weightiness depending on the time and country you live in. I could go on and on with examples. The point is, they are just words so don't get too freaked out about it if your kids say one. Just correct it and move on.

Funny Anecdote: Joe's parents just texted to warn me that he has started to say "Oh, fuck." They are wisely giving it no attention and finding new words to replace it such as "Oh, shucks" and "Oh, man!"

Dress Code

*a*s I said before, the goal is that they are dressed and that they dress themselves. Particularly when they were little, I didn't sweat their style too much. I didn't like it, but I didn't really care either. It was also kind of fun to watch the evolution of it all. I would nudge their style this way and that way by buying things that I'd like to see them in, but they wore what they wanted. I knew not to buy Daniel shirts with buttons. They bothered him. Joshua prefers his pants and shorts to have elastic waistlines. I didn't see any reason to make them wear something they weren't comfortable in. My mom would say, "I wish that the boys would wear _____." Even though I agreed it was a cute look, I wasn't going to push them into anything they didn't like.

I would request they dress nicer if we were eating out somewhere nice (Joshua always loves fancy dining) or if we were going to an event that called for it. When we went on vacations, I would ask them to not pack t-shirts with a character or words on it. I just thought our vacation pictures looked better without it. I can tell you there are pictures of Joshua in a zombie t-shirt, a kilt, knee–high neon–colored socks, and tennis shoes on one of our vacations. *sigh* It got better though.

What about dressing young ladies?

When they are little, let them explore with style. My friend's daughter who dressed like an eccentric bag lady turned out just fine, and she had fun becoming the young woman she is now.

I do recall a tall girl at the elementary school who came to school in tight jeans, high heels, and lipstick. Nope. If I had a daughter, I would not allow this. It's not age appropriate. Like it or not, there are pedophiles who want to sexualize little girls, and they don't need your child's help in the matter. If my daughter wanted to wear high heels and lipstick to school, I'd want to know why. Those things are fine for dress-up at home, but it's not school attire. I should think it's common sense but if one is too young for sex, they are too young to be dressing sexy. Period.

When your daughter starts to wear makeup is entirely up to you. I think I was twelve or thirteen when I got permission, and I made a mess of it. It was still the eighties, and I know blue eyeshadow and magenta lipstick were involved. Then there was a phase of wearing blush for eyeshadow, but I think I kept the magenta lipstick.

When my sister was in fifth grade, she wanted to start wearing makeup. I told her to wear a little blush and lip gloss. It would let her feel like she's wearing makeup and it was subtle enough that Mom and Dad would probably allow it.

It worked!

Sister went through her own awkward makeup experimentation in the nineties. I just remember brown lip liner being a thing.

I have been fortunate enough to have friends with daughters. They would invite me over when the girls got ready for Christmas parties or school dances, and I got to do their hair and makeup. So fun! I've always told them that you want your makeup to enhance your natural beauty. The end result is not to look completely different. One young lady told me that she did want to look completely different.

"Darling girl, you are beautiful and uniquely you. When I'm done with your makeup, you'll still look like you, but your long lashes will pop and your cheeks will look sun-kissed." She was not the prettiest girl there, but she felt great and confident and was able to appreciate some of her features she hadn't really noticed before.

Booty Booty Booty Booty Rockin' Everywhere

The shorts are getting shorter, the pants are getting tighter, and then there's leggings. This will be a delicate segment to write about.

When the kids were in middle school, I drove the carpool for about three families and so my car was coed. At the beginning of the school year, a couple of the girls got in the car and ranted about the misogynistic dress code. The big upset was that the code required that shirts must be long enough to cover their butts when wearing leggings.

"This singles out the girls," they argued.

"Does it say that boys can wear leggings without a long shirt?"

"Well, no, but boys don't wear leggings."

"Imagine if they did," I said. "Just picture it. Now would you like them to wear a shirt that covered their butts and their bulge in the front?"

"Ewwwwwww!"

"Exactly. I know you don't have a bulge, but leggings leave little to the imagination in the booty and vag areas more so for some girls than others. The school can't say, 'Your shirt can be shorter if you have the right kind of body for leggings.'"

My family and I went to Italy one summer. It is *hot* in the summer, and we were there during an unusually high heat wave. There are strict dress codes for visiting the Vatican and other holy places. Though they were unairconditioned, there were to be no bare arms or legs. So we were *schweaty*. A very schweaty family.

When we melted back out onto the streets of Rome we saw scantily clad Italians everywhere, doing what they could to beat the heat. The young women had on booty shorts. These are shorts that are so short in the back that their "booty yams" were exposed.

I made some comment about it, probably something like, "Good grief. Everywhere I look there's booty." Daniel was seventeen at the time and he said, "I don't blame them. It's so hot out here. If it were acceptable for men to wear them, I would." We all laughed at the idea and got gelato.

This conversation came up again with the neighbors, and their daughter said something about how women should be able to dress however they want and that men need to be in control of themselves.

She's right and she's wrong. How a woman dresses is not an invitation to a man to ogle her or touch her. However, studies show that men are more responsive to visual sexual stimuli than women.

From an *IJIR: Your Sexual Medicine Journal* article published January 10, 2013: "Male adolescent boys frequently feel strong genital responses to visual stimuli while adolescent girls' sexual feelings often arise from emotional reactions to their partner, or romantic themes in films, novels, and magazines."

With that in mind, I fully support a school dress code *particularly* in middle school when these young men are having involuntary erections. It's a distraction from learning that they are too young and inexperienced to deal with just yet. I'm not talking about how they behave toward a seductively dressed young woman; they are absolutely in control of that response. But they are not skilled in controlling the biological response. The blood has left the brain and learning is on hold.

So, like cussing and alcohol, I'd probably have the rule that, when you are an adult, if you'd like to dress sexy that is up to you. An underaged person has no reason to be presenting themselves as sexy. Like makeup, let your clothes be flattering to your body without overexposing it.

More About Clothes, Piercings, and Tattoos

Whether it's fair or not, the fact of the matter remains that you will be judged by your appearance. Time and time again you will learn that you shouldn't judge a book by its cover. The scary–looking pierced, tattooed guy in leather may be a grandpa of eight and the sweetest teddy bear you've ever met. Why do we judge by appearances?

It's actually a human survival mechanism. The mind gathers information from experience and from the messages that the tribe (society) sends us and quickly makes an assessment of a person. Going back again to the primitive human, this would be used to decide if an approaching person was of the same family or tribe and if they were safe.

It's important to teach this to your kids because piercings and tattoos are mostly permanent. I just love how a young adult with eyebrow studs, bull nose ring, and neck tattoo is incensed and surprised that no one will hire them due to their appearance. Seriously? Dress for the job you want.

I don't actually have a problem with tats and piercings (though my sons do), but I would make sure while growing up that my kids know if they do get them, put them in places that still make them employable. My friend would tell his daughters, "You don't put a bumper sticker on a Bentley!"

Teach your child how to dress for an interview. Even if it's at Starbucks, you should interview in something a step nicer than holey jeans and a hoodie.

Anything goes with hairstyles because it's just hair. It's not permanent. Hair length and hair color is so fun to change, especially before they have to start having jobs. Let them have fun and express themselves.

Side Note: *Most* everyone I know who got a piercing other than in the ears did not keep them past the age of thirty. The tongue ring, the nose rings, the eyebrow rings, the stud in the neck, the belly button ring, and the nipple ring . . . all gone. Most, not all. I can think of some friends with nose rings. If I had a cute nose, I would totally want one of those.

Sex, Drugs, and Rock & Roll

LET'S TALK ABOUT SEX

I am a big believer in answering your kids' questions as honestly as possible. This does not mean they need all the details of everything, but you can craft an age–appropriate response to just about anything. Not only about sex but regarding other tough subjects like death or divorce as well. Honesty is best.

When Daniel was about four years old, he asked me how babies got in a woman's tummy. I told him that God put them there. That was it. He did not ask for more information than that. If you don't believe in God, you can tell them that love put them there. This is age–appropriate honesty.

That honesty includes not giving genitals pet names. Girls have a vagina and boys have a penis. No one has a leelee or lala except for maybe a Teletubby. There's a story on the web where a little girl kept telling her teacher that her uncle touched her cookie, and it wasn't until later that the teacher realized her "cookie" was a nickname for her vagina. That is reason number one to not give genitals pet names.

Also, if a child says to a potential abuser, "Don't touch my penis!" it is clear to them that this child knows the correct adult terms and will be more likely to tell an adult of any abuse. A child who uses the correct words is empowered.

Starting to use these words at a young age will make The Sex Talk easier when they are older. You'll be more comfortable, and they'll be more comfortable for this important discussion.

I recently talked to a dad who said his daughter had her "p-word."

"Her what?"

"Her 'p-word.' "

"Do you mean her period?"

Turns out that that was exactly what he meant. Then he bemoaned the fact that, now, his daughter and her mother were having secret conversations he's not allowed to be in on.

"Well, yeah, dude. She can't talk to you about her period because you aren't even comfortable saying the word."

Fathers, read this part out loud: vagina, period, tampon, breasts, cramps, menstruation, menopause.

Mothers, read out loud: penis, testicles, pubic hair, wet dreams, sex, orgasm.

Nothing you just said was a bad word. They are body parts and biological actions. Making it more than that has an ill effect on how your children think and feel about these things as adults.

Oh, and "nipple." Everyone has nipples. Everyone say, "Nipple." Very good.

Sex Education

I think it's great that the current statistics on sex show that teenagers are having less of it. This is correlated to being educated on sex in school.

It is a parent's job to teach their child about sex above anyone else's. Unfortunately, not every parent is like you and cares enough about their role as a parent to read a parenting book, let alone to teach their child about sex. Because of this, I am a big supporter of sex education in schools.

When I was in high school a guest speaker came to one of my classes to talk about sex education. He told us about "pearl necklaces" and "golden showers" and other sex acts (if you don't know what those things are, Google them. There's a Who down in Whoville that can explain it to you).

My teacher sat at her desk sort of hidden behind her computer quietly dying. She later learned that this man who was going to various high schools to give these sex talks was a sex predator. This was a fluke incident, but I feel like parents think "pearl necklaces" and "golden showers" are what's being taught in sex education.

Your teachers are teaching your kids about the changes that their bodies are going to go through. They will teach the science of reproduction and how sex creates life. Yes, they'll teach about masturbation. They may even talk about homosexuality. *gasp*

My advice is that *you* get the curriculum, so you'll know what's going to be taught. It is then *your* job to talk to your child about what will be discussed in class.

Once your child learns about sex, they will immediately start having sex. Lots of it. They will learn about homosexuality and will decide to give that a whirl.

That, of course, is not true. They need to learn about these things because they are true and they are reality and they are happening whether you keep it from them or not. Whatever your opinions or personal beliefs are on the matter is for you to teach your child.

One day I was out running an errand and when I got home the house was . . . weird. My husband came up the stairs and we greeted one another and it was . . . weird.

"What's going on?" I asked. "Did something happen while I was gone?"

Turns out he had The Talk, and it was so awkward that it

filled my home with embarrassment. I then saw my son who looked ashen.

"Hey, bud. You okay?" I asked.

"Not really."

"Want to talk about it?"

Surprisingly, he did. He was horrified about what his father had told him and through teary eyes he said, "I can't believe that you let Dad do that to you! *Twice!*"

I died laughing as I hugged him. "Oh, honey . . . he's done it way more than twice."

"Argh!"

I told him it was appropriate for him to be disgusted by sex right now because he's not old enough for sex yet. I assured him that it's fun, especially when it's with someone you love.

I ended the conversation with this advice: "In the future, if you have questions about sex, maybe you should just come and talk to me about it."

One of my friends told me that her son had a lot of questions about sex at a young age. Her friend told her, "He's just curious. Just answer yes or no." She quickly realized that her son was a little more than curious when he asked, "What's a blow job?"

"No."

She said it was then she knew she'd need to give honest answers or otherwise her son would get stupid answers from his stupid friends. This is so true. I once had to explain a BJ to a grown and married woman who literally thought that she should blow. Like you blow a horn. Her parents did her wrong . . .

Masturbation and Virginity

Well, this should be a fun segment.

Let me start by again directing you to Dr. Kevin Leman. He wrote a book titled *Sheet Music: Uncovering the Secrets of Sexual Intimacy in Marriage.*

A reminder that Dr. Leman is a family psychologist. He wrote the book because he had many clients struggling with sexual intimacy. I'm also going to mention that he is a Christian. I think it's important to note that, because we Christians have made sex so sacred and masturbation so sinful that it has created generations of people who have shame and intimacy issues. Dr. Leman saw a lot of this in his practice and wrote this book for married and engaged couples, but I thought it would be worth a read as a parent as well.

The Sex Talk shouldn't be a one–time rite–of–passage sort of thing. It should be an ongoing conversation with your children, starting with using the actual names of body parts and not shaming them when they touch or expose themselves. Be more matter of fact about it all because it *is* a matter of fact. It's a fact that they have genitals, and it feels good to touch them.

If your young daughter raises her dress over her head, there's no need to respond as though it's some great scandal. Just tell her to put her skirt down.

Your child may find that touching themselves feels good when they are little and are taking a bath. What a perfect time and place for such a thing. You'll want to make sure they know that it's only for private times and only for themselves to touch.

You may say, "Michal . . . masturbation is a sin." Is it? The Bible does not say anything about the act of masturbation. There are a handful (pun intended) of Bible verses that have been inter-preted to be about masturbation but no actual Scriptures to say it's wrong.

What Dr. Leman says about masturbation is that you can't play the instrument without first practicing it. He also encourages engaged couples to masturbate (alone, not together) if they are planning to wait for sex until they are married.

I think it's healthy to take the shame of masturbation away and give your child privacy to do so. We also need to stop making virginity so damn sacred. I'm again going to address religion here because that's where this stems from.

Biblically you hear about virginity, primarily pertaining to women. Marriage was more of a business transaction at the time, and a virgin was likely a younger woman who had lots of baby-making years ahead and so was valued more.

Oftentimes the biblical virgin can be translated to simply mean an unmarried person. Men in the Bible really only seem to be committing sexual sin if they are sleeping with another man's wife. In other words, he is using someone else's property. That is sinful and bad. If a woman does the same thing, she is a whore and should be stoned to death.

So now we have this very pure and valuable woman who is a picture of virtue and innocence. Once she's married, she is to suddenly to be a sex goddess for her husband. No wonder Dr. Leman's phone was ringing!

When you are told from a young age to preserve your virginity and that your "hoo-ha" is not to be touched, not even by you . . . yeah. You might have some struggles with opening up to your partner, especially if you're marrying a young man who has been bottling up all of his desires and is ready to pounce on his bride. Yikes!

Consider the culture in which the Bible was written. Consider that they married at a very young age. Now consider that many aren't getting married now until they are thirty or older. With no masturbation or premarital sex. Yeah, right.

I'm not suggesting or advocating that we encourage our kids to be promiscuous; there are physical and emotional consequences to that. Teach them those consequences without making sex shameful or overly sacred.

Funny Story: One of my friends wanted to surprise her husband with a gift of a trench coat. To make it fun, she waited until her three-year-old daughter was in bed, then she got naked and put on the coat. Her husband was watching TV in the basement. Her daughter was sound asleep, so she went downstairs and gave her husband his new coat.

The hot delivery had just the right effect and soon her husband was naked as well and a fun time was being had on the basement couch. In the middle of the fun time, their little girl came down the stairs. Her husband freaked out and started yelling at his daughter, "Get back in bed! Get back in bed!" My friend quieted her husband and calmly told her daughter that she needed to go to bed.

"But why are you naked?"

"Because I was hot."

"But then why is Daddy on top of you?"

"Because then I got cold."

"Just get back in bed!" her husband yelled again.

My friend did the right thing. She knew if they overreacted, this scene would forever be remembered by her toddler. Now that her daughter is an adult, they've told her the story and she doesn't remember the incident at all.

Gender Norms and LGBTQ Kids

When Daniel was in preschool, he was sent home for making a gun with his hand and saying, "Pew, pew." The school reminded me they were a zero–tolerance school, and if my three-year-old did anything like that again he would have to be expelled.

So much of this is hilarious. At this stage my kids did not have toy guns or swords or light sabers. They watched *Baby Einstein*, *Backyardigans*, *The Wiggles*, and things of that nature. I don't know where my son learned this, but I told the school that asking a little boy to not play "guns" is like asking a little girl not to play "house."

You can be mad about it if you want, but there absolutely are things that boys will gravitate to and that girls will gravitate to. Our primitive makeup wires men to hunt and women to gather.

Some gender norms are taught and part of it is innate. All of it is for everyone.

Men are also daddies, so don't be weird about getting your little boy a baby doll. Women can do anything a man can so don't be weird about getting your daughter a BB gun.

Little Joe loves to sit on the bathroom vanity while I get ready. He plays with my makeup brushes because at eighteen months old he already knows there's a drag queen inside.

JOKING! He plays with the makeup brushes because he's in scientist mode and they are so soft. The anthropologist in him is going to mimic what he sees others doing. He tries on my jewelry too. I tell him how handsome he is! With mascara and bracelets on, he gets his wooden tools and starts to hammer and tinker.

My sons have BB guns, so my neighbor got his daughters BB guns and now they are so masculine.

JOKING! They are great shots and look super cool shooting in a dress.

I'm just saying there's nothing to be afraid of. A lot of who your child will be is pre-written in their DNA. Remember the shepherd with the rod? That's us. We're just steering them along the path of life.

I remember a little redheaded boy in third grade who was different. I didn't know why he was different, but he was. He was not like the other boys. He was more like us girls. Sometime in middle school I learned what homosexuality was. I'd heard the word "gay" thrown around (usually as an insult), but I didn't know what it was exactly.

After learning what it was to be gay, I suddenly knew why the little redheaded boy was different.

What if your child is not falling in line with gender norms? What if they are gay? What if they are transgender, gender fluid, pansexual, etc.? You'll love them anyway. Even if you're of the mindset that it's an abomination (this is your kid, remember) you better love that child. Too many young people are committing suicide due to shame and loneliness.

I know many people who were sent to Pray the Gay Away camps. They are still gay. More surprisingly, they are still Christians.

Not quite the same thing, but my kids are nerds, man. Like, *big* nerds who don't move their arms when they run and don't cuss and play tabletop games and live–action reenactment kind of nerds. My sons have worn kilts to school. In *middle school.* I was so impressed with their courage. They are so *proud.* They love their weirdness and their weird friends. Dudes . . . I can't even tell you about all of the friends' weirdnesses.

I have made sure they know I love everything about them (even though I kind of wish they were cooler) and they are proud of themselves too. Every child should have that.

When Daniel was in high school, he joined a Gay Alliance Club. I asked him about it and why he had joined.

"In middle school people will say 'gay' like it's a negative thing. Like, 'that's so gay' meaning that it's lame or stupid. Being accused of being gay was always a negative thing. I was starting to think that maybe I was becoming a bit homophobic. I know that fear of something usually comes from ignorance, so I wanted to educate myself."

"Wow, son. That is exactly right. Tell me about the club. What do y'all do?"

"Mostly the gay kids talk, and the straight kids listen. One girl said she came out to her mom while cooking dinner. They were making spaghetti and as she put the pasta in the boiling water she said, 'Uncooked spaghetti is straight. I'm more like cooked spaghetti.'"

"That was a clever way for her to say that. You know, if you are cooked or uncooked spaghetti, I'll love everything about you."

"Mom . . . I'm straight," he said with a slight eye roll.

"Just . . . being available."

I'm not going to argue whether LGBTQ are sins or not. This book isn't about that. It's about our goal as a parent and how to achieve that goal. That goal, again, is to raise healthy, happy, functional *adults*.

A child who has been told they are an abomination and a deviant by the very people who should be loving them unconditionally will not grow up to be a happy and healthy adult. Not fully. They will have wounds and scars that they can recover from, but a child's pain and trauma should not come from their parents.

The suicide and homeless rate among LGBTQ teens is statistically higher than that of straight teens. This is largely in part to being shamed and/or kicked out by their parents. So you can embrace your LGBTQ teen or run a high chance of having no child to embrace at all.

Loving them does not mean "fixing" them. It does not say "I love you *but*."

- Love *never gives up*.
- Love cares more for others than for self. This isn't about you. It's about your kid.
- Love doesn't want what it doesn't have. What do you have? You have a gay child.
- Love doesn't force itself on others. That includes your beliefs.
- Love is not easily angered. If you are angry by this situation, ask yourself why.
- Love doesn't keep score of the sins of others.
- Love always *protects*. LGBTQ teens and adults will have a lifetime of struggle and hate from society. Your home should be a safe place from that.
- Love perseveres to the end.

(Paraphrased from 1 Corinthians 13:4–8 from
NIV and The Message)

This starts before they are teens. I will not make Joe feel bad for playing with makeup or playing with a doll. I would not shame a girl for being a tomboy either.

Be available. Listen. Love them. That's all most kids need regardless of sexual orientation or gender identity. If you can't help them navigate something, get a therapist your child can talk to and get one for yourself.

Pro Tip: I remember watching the news with my mom as a child and there had been a murder and I voiced how awful the murderer was. My mom said, "He's someone's son. There's a mom out there who is devastated by this news." Then she said, "No matter what you do, I will always love you. I might be disappointed or hurt, but there's nothing you can do to make me stop loving you."

That's what it's all about, Charlie Brown. Your child may have a different political alignment from you or a different faith from you. *You. Never. Stop. Loving.*

Daniel says: Daniel has read this book and he says he wishes I'd talked to him about homosexuality earlier than I did. I usually waited for my kids to ask me questions to answer them, and I had assumed he knew about homosexuals as I have gay and lesbian friends.

He said, "Well, I knew those two women were married, but I didn't know they were gay!"

Just Say No

Now is a good time to talk about drugs. I have some good news. According to the National Center for Drug Abuse Statistics, illicit drug use in teens eighth grade to twelfth is lower than it has been in the past two decades. Alcohol is responsible for the deaths of more young people than all other drugs combined. That being said, underage drinking has also seen a significant decline in recent years. Marijuana is the next drug of choice for teens after alcohol. In states where recreational cannabis is legal, there is less use by teens.

Why? Just like the decline in sex, our kids are more educated on the matter than previous generations. Talk, talk, talk to your kids about these things Don't talk about the sinfulness of it. Talk about the consequences of it. Drugs and alcohol impair judgement, some are addictive, all are *illegal* to the child. Legal trouble is no good.

A kid at the high school got busted for having alcohol and weed in the trunk of his car. Learning opportunity! I talked to my son about it and warned him about the consequences that come from this situation.

"If you try drugs or alcohol, please be smart about it. Do it at someone's home and stay there. The trouble comes when you leave with drugs or alcohol in your system or on your person. Also, in regard to sex. If you're going to do it, *use protection*."

"So . . . you're basically giving me permission to do drugs and have sex," the smartass said.

"Absolutely, not. I know you and would truly be surprised if you did any of this, but I'm your parent and it's my job to keep you safe. A lot of teens will experiment with drugs and alcohol. You are a teen and you're my teen. If you try it, do so safely. It would surprise you to know that I did not drink in high school. Your father, however—"

"*What?* Dad?"

"Yes. Your father. I didn't really start drinking until I had kids. By the way, if you ever do come home drunk or high, there will be hell to pay." (Probably not. I mean, I'd need to know the whole story, but I like to keep them on their toes).

The long–term effects of sex and drugs are what we really want to avoid. Addiction, overdose, driving under the influence, jail, STDs, and unwanted pregnancies. That's where the focus should be when teaching your kids about these things.

You may have been wanting a little more about how to handle things like drugs and rebellion but doing the hard stuff with setting healthy boundaries, creating respect, and allowing natural consequences to discipline your child really helps avoid this sort of thing. Not a guarantee, but it sure helps.

Oftentimes a child who is more into drugs/alcohol beyond experimentation has experienced a trauma that has not been addressed. There's something in life they are wanting to escape. Knowing that could change a parent's approach to handling their child's drug use. It's likely they aren't just being rebellious. There is something much more that needs to be healed.

If your child gets in trouble in this way, the hardest part is to fight the instinct to shield them from the sting of the consequences to follow. This is why we have to let them fall in the little ways when they are young. We have to deliver a consequence when they are still moldable. It's not just a good time for them to learn but it's good practice for us parents when we have to stand out of the way of the discipline that life will deliver.

If/when our kids screw up in big ways, we can still be there for comfort, understanding, and direction but we cannot do much else to change the situation. Nor should we.

Pro Tip: One time, one of my siblings came home wasted drunk. Said sibling's bedroom was by the laundry room. My mom got up early in the morning and put a pair of tennis shoes in the dryer. Excellent way to strengthen the natural consequences her child was experiencing. *KA THUNK! KA THUNK! KA THUNK!*

The Teen Years

*W*hen my kids were little, I had friends who would cry when their child met a milestone or on their birthdays. They mourned each step of their development. They were the good moms who were going to miss "this time."

I rejoiced in every milestone and recognized that every birthday got us closer to the goal. My job as a parent is to work myself out of a job. Eventually, I got a heart and started to cry about some of it. I remember crying when they turned eleven because they were no longer interested in themed birthday parties.

Let us not forget that the goal of parenting is to create a capable, responsible, and good *adult*. It's especially good to remember this when your child is flexing those muscles of independence.

When children are young, they need lots of sleep because they are growing and learning so much. Everyone accepts the Terrible Twos as a difficult phase their child goes through. I think it's important to recall all of that and give that sort of grace when you have a teenager.

Teens sleep a lot too. Not because they are hiding from you or stayed up too late or are on drugs (because you might think that's the reason). They need a lot of sleep because they too are going through massive growing and changing. They too are exhausted from all they are learning. They also may be a bit of a jerk because, like a two-year-old, they are testing out being independent of you.

How Lazy Parents Can Raise an Independent Person

I don't fully believe that mini title because we've already established that parenting is a lot of work. Unfortunate events made me a lazy parent for a time and, thankfully, it worked to the benefit of my children.

A therapist once told me that the three most stressful experiences in life are moving, death, and divorce. The commonality is that they are all times of experiencing loss.

When Joshua was eight months old we moved from Texas to Missouri. We moved back to Texas after twenty-two months and then three years later we moved to Colorado. Every time one moves to a new place it takes two to three years to settle in and shake that feeling of displacement.

Just as I was getting settled into a community and coming out of a fog of depression, we'd move. Though every move has been good for our family, I can look back on old pictures and see the exhaustion and sadness in my eyes.

Moving to Colorado was not just a shock to the system because of another move but because the culture was completely different. We didn't just move to Colorado, we moved to the mountains which is yet even a more different culture than the suburbs and city life of Colorado.

I would cry every time I had to drive in the snow, which was a lot. The mountain area rarely closes down for snow. The style was different. I mean, people were wearing white sandals after Labor Day! I was raised that you were not put together enough to leave the house without blush and earrings on at the very least. Here, everyone was makeup-free. Even professionals eschewed makeup and wore open–toed shoes like Birkenstocks (this was before Katie Holmes was giving a second wind to Birks). They called teachers by their first name. There were only three churches in the whole town. The nearest TexMex restaurant was "down the hill" in the flats. My world was rocked.

Anyhoo . . . just as I was settling into being a mountain woman, my grandma died.

My grandma and I were very close. We talked on the phone multiple times a day. I'd visit her by myself once a year. She was my person. She was the one who could comfort me but also shoot straight with me. She was a good listener. She died the week before I was going to visit her. I missed seeing her by one week.

Emotionally, I was just climbing out of my third bout of depression in six years when she died. With grief, I didn't just experience depression (as one should) but also anxiety. I had insomnia and was a damn mess during the day. It felt like I was in a glass case of emotion. (That's a line from the movie *Anchorman* but it applies. I mean to say that I felt separated from everyone else.) It was so hard to get out of bed. I just moved through a fog. I was mean. My nerves were short. I mean . . . *short*.

I became a yeller again.

This was a terrible time for me and my family, but something good did come out of it. A very odd thing. My children became more independent.

My youngest was seven and my oldest was nine and I struggled to get out of bed. I started having them make their own breakfast and pack their own lunch for school. This is also when I taught them to do their own laundry. I still took them to school and made dinner.

Was this the right time for my kids to be doing those things? I guess so. They did it. They still do it. Suddenly my job as a parent became less laborious. I was still the counselor, the chauffeur, the disciplinarian, etc., but my kids were pretty darn self-sufficient by this point in their lives.

I was not very emotionally available at this time. I remember one time riding in the car with Joshua (I feel like all of these stories are when I'm driving them somewhere) and I had yelled at him for something or another. I think we were late to swim practice because he didn't have his shit together. (My seven-year-old didn't have it together. Ugh. When do we forgive ourselves?). Anyhoo . . . we were in the car, and he put his hand on mine and said, "Mom, I think that maybe you are upset about something else and letting it out on me." Seven. Years. Old.

Now that I think about it . . . he may have gotten that from a line in *Three Amigos,* but he used it correctly. I started to cry and said he was right and apologized for it. I told him I was so sad about my grandma and would try harder to not allow that to affect how I treated him.

With therapy and a prescription of Lexapro, I pulled out of it. However, I allowed my kids to continue making all of their meals except dinner and to do their own laundry.

My husband gave me a Keurig for Mother's Day and it sits on my nightstand. Every morning I wake up to the sound and smell of percolating coffee. I lie in bed sipping my coffee while my children ready themselves for school. Occasionally, I holler out, "Do you have your library book? Did you pack a piece of fruit?"

It was happening, people. They were becoming *independent!*

Proud of You

One time at the airport I overheard two siblings talking. She looked like she was in her twenties, and he was a teenager. Big sister said, "I know Mom and Dad don't ever say it, but I think they are proud of you."

Teen brother grunted.

"Well, even if they're not," big sister said, "I want you to know that I am. I am proud of you. *Okay?*"

Unbeknownst to this young woman, her conversation impacted me. I started to wonder if I'd ever told my sons that I am proud of them. I know I say I love you all the time, but have I told them how proud I was?

Shortly after this trip I decided to make sure I said it. Daniel hugged me and said, "Thanks, Mom. I'm pretty proud of you too."

Joshua responded, "Why? Why are you proud of me?"

Think fast, Michal! I knew "because" wasn't gonna cut it. "Because you're my son" wasn't much better. I needed to be specific.

"I'm proud of who you are and who you will be. I'm proud that you are a good student, but when I hear that you are the kindest kid in school my heart bursts. I love your empathy and sense of humor. You're just awesome!"

I know not everyone says I love you or hugs, but I'm telling you these things are so important. I remember the first time my grandma said, "I love you" to me. I was in my first apartment, and we were getting off the phone. She usually just said, "Good-bye," but this time she added, "I love you." Another "I love you" I recall, similarly, was my aunt. Same thing, signing off on a phone call. That was not strange to hear from one side of my family but from this side it was.

Don't let these things be strange to your children. Say it when they leave, say it when they call, say it after an apology, say it when they go to bed.

Pro Tip: Lovingly touch your children. I once read that a hug is most effective if it's twenty seconds long. That's when oxytocin is released, which is the same hormone released when breastfeeding. This hormone is often called the "love hormone" and helps to reduce anxiety and increase bonding. I taught my family this and every now and then Joshua will say, "Mom, I just need twenty seconds."

The Struggle Bus

Life is hard.

You will never need to create difficulties for your children, nor should you. However, when difficulties arise, you need not step in so quickly to fix things.

For some reason the struggle scenario that comes to mind is learning to tie your shoe. It took forever for my kids to learn to tie their shoes. I still can't stand to watch them tie their shoes because they do it in such an odd way. One of the reasons they tie their shoes weird is because they learned at a late age.

To make my life easier, I'd buy them Velcro shoes. I kept them in Velcro for as long as I could because there was no way we were ever getting out the door on time if they had to tie their shoes. I could've tied them for them but then they'd never learn to get themselves ready and they *still* would not know how to tie their shoes.

I remember learning to do this in kindergarten. We traced our foot on a piece of cardboard and then our teacher put holes in it and laced it with shoestring. She then taught us step by step to tie our shoes, and we had our little foot cutout to practice with.

Learning to tie your shoes is a struggle. Again, allowing this struggle while they are little lets them learn how to cope with struggling when they are big.

Daniel is very smart, precise, and hard on himself. He's a bit of a perfectionist and so he is very deliberate and slow in everything he does from brushing his teeth to driving to doing schoolwork. Slow and steady wins the race. For the most part, making straight A's in advanced classes and having good behavior has come easy for him.

Until he took a physics class with a calculus prerequisite without taking calculus. Did he succeed? Yes. Did he struggle? So, so much! Poor Daniel started questioning everything.

"What's even the point?"

"I don't know, son. I don't know anything about physics."

"No, I mean . . . what's the point? We work hard to get good grades to get into college, so we can get a good job, so we can work, then retire, and die."

"Well, shit. When you put it like that . . . Bub, you're letting one hard class cause you to question life. Even if you make a C in this class, even if you *fail* it, what will happen to you? You will still graduate. You will still get a scholarship even. Try your best but allow yourself to mess up. I promise you this will not define your whole life."

Daniel did graduate and he did get a scholarship and I can't even recall what grade he ended up with in that class.

So now he is in college and the first semester was pretty easy overall. Second semester brought a new challenge.

"I think I should drop this class."

"Why?"

"Because this assignment is really difficult, and they changed the due date on it and I haven't even chosen what I'll do for the project."

Oh, my stars. Long story short, a couple of times in this class Daniel felt too overwhelmed to even start the projects assigned. Once he actually started them, he was finished with them on time, if not in advanced time. The difficulty had him stuck though. He always wanted to drop the class or even change his major. Every time, I'd talk him down and also refuse to let him drop the class.

"What happens if you don't get an A?"

"I could lose my scholarship."

"And?"

"And then I don't know."

"And then dad and I will help you pay for school. When you get a job, your employer will never ask what your scores were. They likely won't even care what college you went to, and they won't care how you paid for school."

I think I failed this one. Somehow I did not allow him to struggle enough.

School was not easy for me. Well, that's not true. I barely studied and made B's and C's. College was very hard for me because I actually did need to study but didn't know how. I worked three part-time jobs to pay for the part of school my student loan didn't cover.

I want to balance this struggle. He is fortunate enough to not have to pay for school but the learning part . . . that's all on him.

Now I'm rambling and sort of swirling in disappointment with myself as a parent. I never should've bought those Velcro shoes.

The Value of a Dollar

When I was growing up, we did not get a monetary allowance. We were allowed to live rent-free, so doing chores was not something my parents owed me money for. That and I don't think they had spare money to offer us anyway.

I started working when I was eleven and became a babysitter. When I was in high school, I worked at a hardware store one year and a clothing store another. I also worked at an office filing and eventually got a job as a sterilization assistant in a dental office.

Why was I working? I'm really trying to recall why I started to work, and all I can think of was that we just really didn't have a lot of money so if I wanted to do something or buy something I needed some cash. In high school the goal was to save money to buy a car and be able to pay for gas and car insurance.

We also did not give the boys allowance for doing chores. I feel that we do chores around the house because we're all living here together so we should work together. If I make dinner, they clean it up. I typically make a list of what needs to be done and then ask them to choose two things from it to do.

Daniel earned money babysitting and Joshua sometimes does things for neighbors to earn money. They both would pet sit from time to time. My husband would give them money for making good grades. I wasn't really keen on this but . . . he would give them cash for getting on honor roll and extra if they made straight A's. At the end of the year, if they had stayed on the honor roll all year, they got a bonus.

He said it was because school was their job, and you can earn bonuses for doing a good job. Once they were in high school the money was put directly into their savings accounts. This and birthday or Christmas money were where they got most of their cash. They can spend their money how they want, but when the money's gone, it's gone.

They have both done very well with saving money. My husband made it a point to teach the kids about compound interest both for savings and in life. I had never heard of this so let me explain in case you didn't know either.

Say you put $10,000 into a savings account. The bank pays 2.5% interest (compounded monthly) for leaving your money there. After one year you now have $10,253. Which doesn't seem like a lot more, but after fifty years you have almost $35,000.

The life lesson is the same. The decisions you make as a young person have a compounding effect. They may not seem like a big deal when you're younger, but the compound effect by the time you're in your sixties may be. For example: smoking, drug use, or dropping out of school in the moment may not have a great impact but later in life you recognize that it negatively affects your present.

I asked Joshua what we've taught them about work. He said

he remembered that his dad told him to pick up dog poop in the backyard. Our yard is an acre, and we have three dogs. It's hard and gross work. He asked, "What's the point of doing this?"

His dad said, "Because in life you'll have to work hard to get what you want." Basically, life is hard so we aren't going to allow it to be easy all the time.

Communicating with a Teen

For years you've been wishing they'd stop talking and stop asking so many questions. Don't worry, your teenager will gladly grant you that wish.

Now it's the teenager who is wishing you'd leave them alone and stop asking questions. I have seen this in male and female teens; they start to mumble, and they close off in their bedrooms. They also get snarky and tend to speak with a tone of disrespect.

After all the work you've put in when they are young this will still happen. It's part of growing up and becoming independent. Keep in mind that your child disagreeing with you is not disrespectful. *How* they disagree with you can be.

Teens are thinking deeper and developing their own ideas about things, and some of it may be different from yours. That's okay. It's a good sign that they are becoming an individual and their own person. Just because they are exploring an idea different than you taught them also does not mean that they will completely abandon any of it, especially if you are respectful about their explorations.

There's a period of time that a baby thinks it's one being with others. Around eighteen months a child may start throwing fits and challenging the rules because they have realized they are separate from you. Similarly, this is what's happening in a teenager.

Understanding what's happening developmentally, you can drop the arguing and punishment and try to reach your teen where they are. Give them the appropriate way to talk to you and to disagree with you. As I've said before, demonstrate positive communication and make sure family rules are clear.

If you're like me and cuss, don't cuss *at* your kids. If you call them names and cuss at them, you can bet they will do the same to you. (I have no doubt my kids just read that and rolled their eyes. Teaching your child to drive does not count in the cursing *at* your child department. It just doesn't.)

Drop the nagging. A reminder is fine but constantly repeating something is going to anger anyone. To let them know it's being left to them I usually say something like, "Hey, you're probably already all over this but I wanted to remind you about that project coming up. Let me know if there's anything you need from me."

If they end up dropping the ball, ask what more would've helped. "I reminded you about it once. Would it help if I gave more frequent reminders? Should we write it on the calendar?" Let them tell you what will work for them. If they later get mad because you "nagged" remind them that this was the game plan *they* created.

Sometimes they'll take offense with the one reminder to which I'd say, "You know, I get it that it's annoying, but you're still my responsibility. It's my job to get you to the finish line."

They are also going to feel defensive at your "invasion of privacy" when you're really just trying to stay connected and be a part of their world. Again, honest conversation is the best way to handle it: "Hey, man. I get it that you're becoming an adult and so you will have your own adult life. Right now, you're still my kid. I like you and I want to know what's happening in your world. You don't have to tell me everything, but when I asked about where you went and who you were with, it was more about striking up a conversation than about checking up on you."

There are times when their disrespect is a concern and is more than your regular teenager flexing their independence muscles. If there seems to be an overt change in personality and attitude, withdrawing from friends or their usual hobbies/interests, running away or drug abuse, professional help may be needed. Therapists, school counselors, and even troubleshooting with other parents can all be ways to overcome the more difficult times with a teen.

Otherwise, don't freak out if your teen is argumentative, standoffish, and more private. Remember that all of the hormones they are experiencing are new. It's causing communication problems and more sensitivity which is frustrating and will likely manifest in anger or rudeness.

The Feels

MENTAL HEALTH

*A*s I mentioned before, I have struggled with depression and with anxiety. The depression, I would say, was pretty situational. It's normal to be emotionally scrambled after a move, even if it's a good one. That and moving with little guys when you are screwing up as a parent . . . it brings you down.

When my grandmother died I was, of course, sad. Due to the surprise of it and the fact that I was preparing to go and visit her, followed by wildfires near my home, some anxiety kicked in.

A little layman's explanation for what happens when you have anxiety: When the primitive man was in danger, adrenaline would gush through the body so he could fight or run (fight or flight). Primitive man was dealing with things like a saber tooth tiger, say. Most of modern man's stress is traffic, work, or busy schedules. Then there are the bigger stresses like moving, death, divorce, forest fires.

When one experiences a trauma (and what's trauma for one person may not be for another) the body releases adrenaline in much the same way as it did for the primitive man. However, there's no tiger on one's tail. One can't physically do anything about most modern stressors.

What I experienced with anxiety was adrenaline that had no output. This then manifested in physical problems like IBS, sleep apnea (they say it doesn't but soldiers with PTSD may differ), insomnia, tics, trouble swallowing, twitching muscles, rashes, difficulty breathing, little electric prickles all over my body, and numbness on my left side. Oh, and dry heaving. Not always all at once but . . . pretty much all at once. The emotional response wasn't constant worry but anger.

I saw many doctors and specialists in regard to all the different physical issues. They could never find an actual problem though they could see and believed me that these things were happening. I thought I was losing my mind. I would've been relieved to be diagnosed with a brain tumor so there was at least an explanation and something that could be attacked.

I finally said to one doctor, "Look, I'm having lots of different problems and they seem to not be 'real.' Could it all be anxiety?"

To which this good woman said, "Absolutely," and recommended a therapist.

I did a lot of therapy which helped me understand so much about my response to my grandmother's death but also other past traumas. This was great. Understanding was good as it helped me respond to present things differently, but nothing fixed the physical problems until I started taking anxiety medication. Some of the things I listed completely went away and others pop up every now and then when, oh, say, there's a worldwide pandemic or people attack the United States Capitol.

Where am I going with this?

Growing up, anxiety wasn't really a "thing," but depression was the new diagnosis getting thrown around. The talk around clinical depression was not positive. People with depression needed to pray it away, choose to be happy, were crazy, lazy, and ungrateful.

Taking medication for it was for the weak who were choosing to not fix themselves. However, therapy was also a negative thing. Therapy was for crazy people and was full of hocus pocus.

Being clinically depressed is when you are depressed for no reason. Depressed because someone died is normal. Depressed because you lost a job is normal. When everything improves but you're still depressed . . . there might be a problem.

As I was experiencing all of these physical ailments due to anxiety, I started to recall seeing some of this in others when I was growing up. I also saw some of this in my kids.

After our move to Colorado, one of the boys would wake up sick to his stomach every morning before school. He'd dry heave as he walked to the bus stop. I thought he was just trying to get out of going to school. Now I was realizing that he was going through the same emotional scramble that I did after moving. The other son would have a tic of some sort, usually throat clearing, every time a new school year would start.

It hit me that one day my kids may need therapy or medication for mental health issues, and I needed to make it . . . well, not an "issue."

I started letting them know what was going on with me. "After school, I'll drop you off at home but then I have an appointment with my therapist."

"What? You go to *therapy?*"

"Yeah," I'd say nonchalantly.

"Why? Are you . . . crazy?"

"Well, surely you already knew that," I joked. "I'm not seeing a therapist because I'm crazy but because I'm having a hard time working through Grandma's death. You know how I've been short-tempered and the dry heaving in the mornings . . . that's all because of that. Honestly, I think everyone needs to see a therapist just like you see a dentist."

"Oh. So like, every six months?"

At the time I was going much more frequently than every six months but . . . yeah. Ha!

When I started to take medication for anxiety, I told them and they noticed the change in me and they were thrilled.

Fast-forward to Daniel's carjacking.

Street Smarts!

Daniel was a highly sought–after babysitter. He watched two kids over the summer. On the last day of summer break, their mom gave Daniel permission to take the kids to an amusement park. On the way to the amusement park they were at a stoplight when Daniel witnessed a car do a "Tokyo drift" through the intersection and then wreck into another vehicle. Shortly after, a man came to his passenger window and asked if he could use Daniel's phone to call for help.

Daniel's instinct was to ignore this guy. Something was "off," but he's always been taught to help those in need. He rolled down the window enough to hand the man his phone, but the man pushed the window down farther, reached in to unlock the door, and got in the car.

One thing I have taught my kids is that if a bad guy wants what you have, give it to them and run. Give them your shoes, give them your wallet, give them your car, whatever it is, it is not worth your life. The problem was Daniel had two kids in the back seat that he was responsible for. He could not relinquish the car and leave the kids in danger.

The man reached across Daniel and opened the driver side door and began trying to push him out and take control of the car. He succeeded (sort of) but Daniel was buckled to the car even though his feet were out of the car and on the ground. The man floored the gas. Daniel ran alongside the car and they hit the vehicle parked in front of them. The man tried to climb over my son who wrestled with the perpetrator. Daniel grabbed the dude's shorts and pulled them down as the man tried to run away. The police caught him. Miraculously, my son only suffered a bump on the head, some scratches, and a bruised knee. The kids in the back were also bruised but safe. Their parents said Daniel was the most underpaid babysitter in the world.

One night shortly after that, Daniel asked to speak to me.

"Mom, I think I may need to talk to someone about what happened to me. Like . . . a therapist."

What he didn't know was that I had already called mine and had things in the works.

I don't know if he would've thought to ask this or been comfortable to ask this if I had not spent the previous few years being open and destigmatizing therapy. I also feel partly responsible for not making it clear enough that there are times when it's okay to not be polite.

Teach your kids to trust their instincts. We are the only animal who doesn't. We're the only animal who thinks, "This feels wrong . . . " and then continues to move toward the scary. Like in those dumb horror movies. *Don't go in there!* Our instincts scream but the dumb heads we are, we go right into the danger. Why? Because we have to see it to believe it. We have to be polite and not be judgmental. My therapist taught me that our instincts are right 90 percent of the time. That means there's only a ten percent chance you are being unnecessarily rude to someone who is making you feel uncomfortable.

A friend of mine has a no–sleepovers rule. She firmly believes that nothing good ever happens at sleepovers. Her daughter finally convinced her to allow her to stay the night at a friend's house (this was pre-cellphones). Wouldn't you know it . . . the dad got drunk and was fighting with the mom. Her daughter was super uncomfortable and nervous. When my friend learned what happened she was kicking herself. She had a strong feeling that she should not leave her daughter there. Trust your gut.

Pro Tip: One thing I've always told my kids and their friends is that if they don't feel safe in a place, they can always call me, and I'll get them. They can text me an "X" and I'll call them with a story as to why I have to pick them up. If they are drunk, they can call for a ride home. No questions asked. I wouldn't even be mad.

I really think that's the best way out of some situations. The biggest thing is to not worry about getting out politely. Trust your gut and get away.

Feelings

Part of trusting your instincts comes from being allowed to feel your feelings.

I was often told as a child that I was overly sensitive. My dad called me "Sensitiva" as a nickname (that's "sensitive" in Spanish). I remember being at the dinner table and the family was all teasing one another. In my memory they were all teasing me only, but I want to believe that everyone was probably all teasing one another. However it was going, I was feeling ganged up on and the jokes were cutting too deep. My feelings were hurt. I asked them to stop and was told I was being overly sensitive.

"Oh, come on! We're all just joking. You're being silly/ridiculous."

The refusal to stop and the disregard for how I felt hurt more than the teasing. I started to cry.

"Good grief, stop crying. You're not hurt."

And then my dad said, "This is a teasing family. If you don't like it, you can leave."

Everyone, including myself, burst into laughter at how freakin' ridiculous a statement that was. It became a running joke in the family.

Ha the frickin' ha.

Parents, not only mine, just want some peace and quiet, for the love of Pete! This is one of the reasons kids are often told to stop emoting. Stop crying. Stop laughing. Stop yelling. Stop whining. Some better ways to address that are:

- I see and understand that you're upset. Why don't you go cry it out in your room? I'm here to hug you when you're ready for one.
- Wow, guys! I can tell you're having a lot of fun, but the car is a small space. Let's try to tone it down a bit. I need to at least be able to hear if a fire truck is coming (haha).
- I know you're angry, but I need you to take some deep breaths and find a better way to express your anger instead of yelling. When you're ready to *talk* to me about why you're angry, let me know, but I will not be yelled at. (Be ready for that to come back to you.)
- I can't understand what you're saying when you whine. Change your tone and tell me again.

There is nothing wrong with having an emotion; it's what we do with it that can be an issue.

Joe has started getting really angry if I tell him no. His response has been to throw something or to even hit me. The response from me has been the same. I grab his hands and say, "Hey. You can be mad at me if you want, but you may not throw things or hit me. It's Time Out."

Then we sit on my couch, and I keep him in my lap without looking at him or talking. There's a little wrestling and angry noises from Joe and I'll acknowledge it once by saying, "It's okay for you to be mad. You can use Time Out to settle down." Because he's not quite two, his Time Out is one minute. When the time is up, I set him down off the couch and he's right as rain.

The other day Joshua almost killed us three times in about five seconds. How? He has a permit to drive. The short version: We crossed a four–lane highway when it was not clear and we were nearly T-boned three times. I screamed like Jamie Lee Curtis, cussed, and prayed all at once.

After we were safe, Joshua burst into tears. He cried so hard he got a bloody nose. I had him pull over. We got out of the car and hugged for twenty seconds. I prayed for him and then we discussed what went wrong. Once home I suggested he go inside and take a long hot shower, cry more if he needed to, and then have a hot cup of tea (Joshua loves hot tea).

A hot shower or bath is a great way to de-stress, don't you think? It works for your kids the same way it works for you. When the kids were babies, I'd sometimes get in with them and just hold them. It also gives an older child alone time to decompress. A nice back rub works too. Not everyone likes to be touched, but your child might like to lie in bed while Mom rubs their back.

Pro Tip: When Joshua was so upset by his bully that he could barely speak, I had him take slow deep breaths until he could talk.

I once had a drama student have a panic attack. I had her go for a walk with me and count her steps. Then we sat down, and I asked her to name three things she could see, three things she could hear, and three things she could touch. When you're anxious it's because you are worrying about the future. Counting things in your current space grounds you in the present.

All of these things are tools that these kids can now use

even as adults. Let's not forget that we are raising them to be adults.

Loss

As I said we had a brief time when my little family moved quite a bit. The first two moves did not affect the kids very much because they were pretty young. The third and final move was a doozy for all of us. Daniel was going into third grade and Joshua was starting first. Aside from the initial hurt and frustration of moving, Daniel bounced back pretty quickly.

Joshua took much longer to get past it. He was sick before school and would fight with me while we got ready. One time when the bus pulled up at the bus stop, he suddenly turned around and tried to make a break back to the house. I thought he was just being difficult like he was when he was a three-year-old. At school he was excellent. His teachers loved him. He was the kindest student in school and had exemplary behavior. At home, he was combative, grumpy, and whiny.

It was my friend, Caren, who pointed out my own emotional struggle that I was having with moving and that Joshua was likely experiencing the same thing. She told me that a lot of times kids will fake it 'til they make it home. Once home, they can stop trying so hard and let it all out in their safe space.

It made so much sense and I adjusted my approach to Joshua's behavior. We'd talk more about what was really bothering him and that it's okay to feel the way he did. I'd encourage him to write letters and draw pictures that we could send to friends and family back in Texas. We also called our loved ones.

Immediately after this move, our very old dog passed away. We'd been here all of three weeks. The day he died, both boys cried and then Joshua started cleaning the house. Why do some people do this? He grabbed the Windex and a washcloth and started cleaning all the windows. In hindsight I see that he was trying to obtain a sense of order and control.

Two years after the move my Grandma died. I remember telling the boys and that they cried a bit but then were kind of excited because we'd be taking a trip to New Mexico for the funeral. I did not know it would be an open casket. Had I known I could've at least prepared myself and especially the kids. Daniel was stoic as usual. Probably stuffing down his negative emotions. Joshua, my sensitive one, lay down on the pew so he couldn't see her, cried, and begged to leave.

Once home everyone returned to work and school. One day Joshua's teacher called and let me talk to him on the phone. He said he felt sick and wanted to come home. I picked him up from school and on the way home I told him that I didn't think he was sick.

"Yes, I am!" he said indignantly.

"I believe you that you feel sick, but I think you're actually sad about Grandma. You're grieving. Grief makes us feel sick. It hurts and we will feel sad and sometimes angry."

"Will I always feel like this?"

"It will feel less hurtful. You'll always miss Grandma and there will be times where that will make you feel sad again. Eventually it will hurt less though. Your heart will heal."

"How? How does it heal?"

"Well, it can be different for everyone, but I think talking about her and remembering the good times helps. I'll tell you what, when we get home, we'll make *natillas*."

Natillas is a Spanish custard that Grandma used to make. It can be served warm or cold. I think it's especially comforting to be served warm. While Joshua and I made her recipe he asked, "Can Grandma see us?"

"I think so."

"Maybe she sees me making *natillas*. I hope she'll be impressed."

"She absolutely is."

After we made and ate the *natillas* I suggested we take a walk.

"Exercise and sunshine are also good for helping your heart heal."

We talked more on the walk, but it was less about Grandma and death and more about what we saw. I think sometimes death does that. You notice everything more vibrantly. You hear the birds. You smell the air. And then there's a time when all of that becomes background again.

Empathy

Both of my sons are incredibly empathetic. When Daniel was carjacked he immediately had concerns for the guy who jacked him. Daniel wanted to be sure he had a way to improve himself while in prison so that he wouldn't come out and repeat the cycle of crime and prison that he was already in. It was important to him that he got his GED, and he was worried whether this young man, who had a child himself, would still have visitation with the child. When COVID hit he kept wondering how this guy was doing and were they keeping the prisoners safe. This man almost killed my son and endangered the lives of two little kids. He doesn't deserve our empathy, but that doesn't mean it's wrong to have empathy for him.

I think some people, like Joshua, are naturally apt to be empathetic and others need to be taught. It can start when they are babies. This is when they look to you to know how to react to something like meeting a new person. Is the babysitter good? You, as a parent, being welcoming to the sitter and calm in the handover will help the baby to know that this is a good person and good place to be. This also helps a baby to start to understand the people around them.

When they are toddlers, they start to understand that they have their own feelings and so do others. They practice making expressions and using them. You're mad? Then I'll smile. You told me no? Then I'll make a sad face and pretend to cry. They've learned that you respond to their emotions.

This is the age to start teaching empathy by talking about it and demonstrating it. When reading books I would point out the expressions of the characters. "Thomas is sad. See his sad face? Let me see your sad face. Now let me see a happy face. Can you make a mad face?"

"Did that noise scare you? It's very loud but not dangerous. I'll keep you safe."

"Ouch! That hurt when you scratched me. That makes me sad. Can you help me find a Band-Aid so we can make it feel better?"

"You made Sarah sad when you took the toy from her. Let's give it back and find something different for you to play with."

As I said before, acknowledging their feelings and not trying to fix or change negative emotions like sadness or anger will foster empathy. Allowing them to feel those things will let them get to know that emotion and understand how someone else feels when they are having that emotion.

The most empathetic kids I know are theater kids. I know I have bias here but kids in theater are stepping into another character's situation. They can imagine what that character is going through and how they would feel in that scene. It's the very definition of empathy.

Ready to Launch

FINISHED

The summer before Daniel left for college, I noticed the light on in his room though it was very late. He was talking on the phone with his girlfriend. I gave a courtesy knock, peeked into his room, and suggested he maybe wrap it up soon and not stay up too late. He firmly said, "No," and gently closed the door. I stood there with my jaw dropped and went to my bedroom where my husband was waiting in bed.

"Your son just told me no," I said with amusement.

"Yeah, well, he's a man now. He doesn't need to be told when to go to bed."

"Ha! He's hardly a man," I laughed. "It hurts a little but also, I love that he's pushing back. He's being independent. Honey . . . I think we did it. I think we've made someone who is his own person. He's ready."

As adults, they will meet their own needs. They will find advice, love, comfort, and support from friends and spouses. If we fostered a good relationship in the brief time we've had with them, we'll be included in that honored place of their inner circle.

While I see parenting as spaghetti, my husband sees it as

compound interest and long–term investments. He's right. Everything we are doing now, everything we are putting into our children now will shape them as well as their children and their children's children. We parents need to keep that idea ever present. We are not just doing momentary troubleshooting with our kids. We are making long–lasting effects in people.

Notes

School Days

1. Joshua read this and is offended. He'd like it known that he also plays Dungeons and Dragons, performs in theater, and is developing a honey of a singing voice.
2. *Name changed to protect the turd.*

About the Author

Michal was raised in Texas alongside her husband of twenty-three years. Together they have raised two truly fabulous humans and now reside in the mountains of Colorado.

In between carpooling and laundry, Michal is involved in the community theaters in her area. She performs, manages, and directs both children's and adult productions.

Michal's main goal has been to raise good people. Her side gig is to entertain or be entertained. Besides theater, she finds joy in party planning, decorating, gardening, and a vast array of other little things.

9 781955 043373